Dedication

This book is dedicated to my family, the Israelites.

Author's Note

As a student of Elder Shadrock Porter, Leader and Master Teacher of the Israelite Nation World Wide Ministries, it is with great honour that I say we adhere to the Israelite religion, the only religion. The God of Abraham, the God of Isaac, and the God of Jacob is the name we call our God, as stipulated in **Exodus 3:15**. We keep the seventh day of the New Moon as a Sabbath. Our book is the authorised 1611 King James Version of the Bible. We believe that the Bible was written by Israelites, for Israelites and about Israelites. We are the authority of this book.

God was the first man. He created Adam in His own image and likeness. He created the earth and Adam was formed from the rich dark soil of the earth. Which means God was Black, Adam was Black, and the Israelites in the Bible were Black as well. However, it is our duty to teach all Nations, including Gentiles, about our Father, who we sometimes refer to as the God of Israel. We do not call Him by any other name but that which was instructed in **Exodus 3:15**.

We follow the first and second testament. We do not refer to Jesus as God, **Hebrews 2:9** clearly identifies who Jesus was, for he **"was made lower than the angels."**

We do not speak what is known today as the Hebrew language, and the reasons why can be found in the section on 'Speaking Hebrew' on page 7. We follow the ordinances written in our book. We have developed and follow the Israelite calendar, which is based on the instructions in our holy book. With our constitution, we have established ourselves as a Nation within a Nation. We have our flag, our coat of arms, our policies and procedures. We have our own building and resting place, etc., and we live and dwell in our own culture.

In accordance with the Scriptures, our foundation is established on the precepts and principles as laid out by the patriarchs, prophets, priests, and apostles of the Israelite Doctrine. Our roots are deeply planted in the soil of prophecy, and that is why we understand. What we do is more than just a momentary practice. We are not just a race of people or a political movement. We are a spiritual people having a human experience, defined by our culture and way of life. We are the true Israelites.

The Hidden Secrets of the True Israelites

By

Dr. Charmain D. Ford | BSc (Hon), MPhil, DID

Officer of the Israelite Nation World Wide Ministries,

Philosopher and Doctor of the Israelite Doctrine

Notice of Copyright

All rights reserved. No part of this publication may be reproduced, distributed, or transmitted in any form or by any means, including photocopying, recording, or other electronic or mechanical methods, without the prior written permission of the publisher, except in the case of brief quotations embodied in critical reviews and certain other non-commercial uses permitted by copyright law. For permission requests, write to the publisher, addressed "Attention: Permissions Coordinator," at the address below.

Edited By:

Elder Shadrock Porter, Master Teacher, Founder and Leader of the Israelite Nation World Wide Ministries

Printed By:

Fifth Ribb Publishing Company

ISBN: 978-1-7367898-0-3

Printed in the United States of America

First Printing Edition, 2021

Copyright © 2020

Table of Contents

INTRODUCTION 1

PHYSICAL IDENTITY 4

SPEAKING HEBREW 7

    There is no such thing as the Hebrew Language 8

    Language in Context 9

  HEBREW TONGUE 12

  ISRAELI HEBREW LANGUAGE 12

  THE NAME OF GOD 15

    The Invention of EBY 16

    Spirit to Spirit 18

  CONCLUSION 20

HISTORICAL IDENTITY 22

  THE IBERIAN PENINSULA 23

  THOSE THAT CALL THEMSELVES JEWS 27

  THE AFRICAN CONNECTION 28

  THE INDIAN CONNECTION 34

  CONCLUSION 36

POST SLAVERY 38

INSURRECTIONS 41

  GABRIEL PROSSER: SLAVE REBELLION - AUGUST 30, 1800 41

    Denmark Vesey: Slave Rebellion - July 14, 1822 41

    Nat Turner: Slave Rebellion - August 21, 1831 42

CULTURAL IDENTITY 44

BLACK NATIONALIST AND BHI MOVEMENTS 48

    Church of God and Saints of Christ (COGSOC) 48

    The Temple of the Gospel of the Kingdom 50

    Church of the Living God 51

    Commandment Keepers 51

    Universal Negro Improvement Association and African Communities League (UNIA)... 53

    The Moorish Zionist Temple of the Moorish Jew... 55

    Beth B'nai Abraham 56

    African Hebrew Israelites of Jerusalem 57

    The Nubian Islamic Hebrews 58

    Israeli School 59

    House of Judah 60

    The Nation of Yahweh... 60

    Israeli Church of Universal Practical Knowledge 61

    The House of David 62

    Cultural Centre of New Covenant Church of Israel... 63

    Israelite Church of God in Jesus Christ 63

    Israel United in Christ (IUIC) 64

    The Israelite School of Universal Practical Knowledge.. 66

    True Nation Israelite Congregation 66

    Sicarii Hebrew Israelites 67

    Israelites Saints of Christ (ISOC) 67

    The Law Keepers 67

    House of Israel 68

    Notable Mentions 69

SPIRITUAL IDENTITY 71

CONCLUSION 76

BIBLIOGRAPHY 78

Introduction

There was a time before slavery, before America, Africa, and Europe, when the descendants of a forgotten people were united. This unity resulted from their belief in a supreme God. In that unity, they were able to establish phenomenal societies of educational and political mastery. Women were held in high esteem, and children were precious; a young girls' virtue was protected, boys were closely guided, elderly men were respected, and young men were admired. This was not the dream within Plato's Republic; this was a reality. Today, within our so-called modern civilisation, we have these same people, now the descendants of slaves, sometimes behaving in the worst possible manner.

The ironic aspect is that there are more philosophies and philosophical establishments than one would care to mention. Yet, the division among the descendants of the children of slavery is unprecedented, and they make up some of the most prominent participants of these religious establishments within western society. Why? Because they have an innate ability to serve. They must serve; the problem is whom they are serving. This book aims to unravel some hidden secrets of the true Israelites.

The descendants of the children of slavery are trying to stand out and make a statement through their natural, yet misguided, musical, artistic and athletic talents. Need I go into the consciousness of a Black man and society's effects? Not today, as this discussion needs a great deal of time to formulate on paper. However, it is evident that the divide is extreme to the point where people do not even bother to discuss Black-on-Black crimes anymore, because it seems so normal that other cultures not only accept it, they expect it. Let us not forget the *Black Lives Matter* movement, which demonstrates that Black lives only matter if there is a case of police brutality of misconduct. What about the elders? It is somewhat challenging to respect elders who do not even know what respect feels like themselves.

For the descendants of the children of slavery, the answer is a lot simpler than discussions on the cosmic consciousness, figuring out the theory of relativity, or earning money with artistic or musical abilities. However, as simple as the solution may be, several factors need to be addressed first; otherwise, it would be a case of leading, albeit, a stubborn and thirsty horse to water that they will not drink.

The first realisation is knowing oneself – okay, another cliché – but think about it. Regardless of the atrocities that they may or may not have suffered throughout history, many nations in this world still can unite for a single cause. The children of slavery will seldom unite because our views on even the simplest concepts are too divided. Most cultures have a belief system, which is the foundation of their existence, regardless of whether they are being educated under different scenarios. Except for the children of slavery, who has gravitated and accepted the teachings of everyone else's philosophy? For example, if you saw a person of East Indian descent, regardless of what they have adopted now, if you asked them what was their traditional beliefs 400 years ago, they will tell you – Buddhism, Islam, Hinduism etc. Even the Europeans had their Pagan philosophies, Christianity and Catholicism, and the Native Indians of America worshipped nature and the spirits of the air. Also, the native Africans will talk about ancestral worship. But ask a child of slavery – well, it would depend on which one you asked – but I guarantee their response would be understandably varied, because most do not know what took place before slavery, and most believe they are from Africa.

Many people in this world can identify with a shared history of their ancestry. I have met descendants of slaves that refuse to speak of slavery. They are often disgusted with this notion to the point of dis-associating themselves from such discussions. Accordingly, when it comes to slavery, we should "get over it,", yet we are constantly reminded of other nations' events. They speak with pride and admiration of their ancestors' courage and celebrate their successes and use it as a building block to propel them to victory. From Mexico to China, they have a day set aside to honour and remember their dead, and they take this tradition as serious as life itself – not to say this is the answer for the children of slavery. Also, the Ashkenazi Jews will never forget or let the world forget their holocaust. Consequently, in 2019 during the 400th anniversary since the first Africans were brought to the shows of Virginia, not one world dignitary, president or prime minister went to Virginia to commemorate this historic moment. Yet dignitaries and world leaders rally together on a yearly basis to commemorate the Ashkenazi Jews holocaust.

The second realisation is of identity; this covers the same points mentioned earlier. However, what tends to happen is that if and when there is a realisation of self, most descendants of the children of slavery tend to gravitate towards African ancestral worship, Egypt, Ethiopia and Nubia, for a sense of Black pride. These were some of the most powerful civilisations of their time, and some of them were known as the enemies of the God of the Israelites. Not all Black people are the same or have the same culture, history or identity.

Additionally, few of these conscious descendants of the children of slavery are aware of the tremendous Israelite kingdoms and societies outside of Jerusalem and Israel; some lasted for hundreds of years before their final demise. More people are becoming aware of the traditions that continue throughout western Africa, which are the traditions of the Israelites that were once settlers of these regions, practices including circumcision and naming of a boy child on the eighth day, or the separation of clean and unclean during certain spiritual events. These traditions are even carried out in certain West Indian and South American countries, countries where the children of Israel were taken to during their nightmare voyage to the new world.

There is a movement that has been taking place, which started around the time of the insurrections of the 1800s. This movement morphed into the civil rights movement of the 1960s and now has taken on a more radical, almost conscientious, approach to the Black nationalist movement. These groups are known as the Black Hebrew Israelites (BHI) and often go by a plethora of names and are from several different camps of various teachings. These groups seem to change their teachings on a whim and, more often than not, have secretly harboured the teachings of Elder Shadrock Porter, Master Teacher and founder of the Israelite Nation World Wide Ministries. Nevertheless, their response and actions are physical, mirroring that of their Black nationalist past, and they seem to lack the spiritual amplitude required to teach the doctrine of truth. Like those of the Christian churches of former years, most of the BHI members are members because it is a place to belong and a prominent part of the quest for identity.

The realisation of self and identity are discussed at length in four chapters relating to the physical, historical, cultural and spiritual identity of the descendants of the children of slavery. In Chapter One: we examine *Physical Identity* by investigating some crucial aspects belonging directly or indirectly to this notion of identity, including language and how it impacts spirituality. And, why we should have nothing to do with the Israeli Hebrew Language. In Chapter two we take a look at *Historical Identity* to clarify how the children of Israel ended up in Western Africa and why returning to or identifying with Africa is a mistake. Additionally, returning to Israel, the land is also a grave mistake and goes against the biblical prophecies. Chapter Three looks at *Cultural Identity* and we take a deep dive into the Black Nationalist and Black Hebrew Israelite movement and how some of their rhetoric is misleading and contrary to biblical teachings. Finally, even though *Spiritual Identity* is the guiding principle throughout this book, this book would not be complete without looking at the spiritual ramification of the descendants of the children of slaves.

Chapter One

Physical Identity

Most of the individuals, organisations, and groups discussed in this book have one thing in common: They believe the people of the Bible were Black. The Black identity is evident through the following scriptures.

As mentioned previously, God created man in his image and likeness from the soil of the earth.

"And God said, Let us make man in our image, after our likeness… So, God created man in his own image, in the image of God created he him; male and female created he them." -Genesis 1:26-28

"And the Lord God formed man of the dust of the ground, and breathed into his nostrils the breath of life; and man became a living soul." -Genesis 2:7

Their identity was and still is crucial. **"And Adam lived an hundred and thirty years, and begat a son in his own likeness, and after his image; and called his name Seth" -Genesis 5:3**

Next, we consider Moses, a Black man, born in Egypt, found and raised by Pharaoh's daughter, and the only way she could tell him apart from her people was because Moses was circumcised. Further, evidence to Moses' identity came years later when he came face to face with God and asked for a sign.

"And the Lord said furthermore unto him, Put now thine hand into thy bosom. And he put his hand into his bosom: and when he took it out, behold, his hand was leprous as snow. And he said, Put thine hand into thy bosom again. And he put his hand into his bosom again; and plucked it out of his bosom, and, behold, it was turned again as his other flesh." - Exodus 4:6-7.

His hand turning white was enough to show Moses, to whom he spoke. **Leviticus 13** talks about leprosy symptoms on the skin, the signs to seek, and the remedy for the problem. Moses married an Ethiopian woman who was Black, in **Numbers 12:1**. Miriam had an issue with Moses marrying outside of his people. She also had a problem with his relationship with the God of Israel, resulting in her physical chastisement. The rest of **Numbers 12** speaks to how Miriam became leprous, **"white as snow."** It also demonstrates her separation as per the laws in **Leviticus 13**.

King Solomon said, **"I am black but comely,"** in **Song of Solomon 1:5-6**. Job said, **"My skin is black upon me"** in **Job 30:30**. Naaman's leprosy and miracle cure is mentioned in **2 Kings 5**. In the book of Daniel, God's hair was compared to wool. In Revelations, there are extensive descriptions of Jesus the Christ:

"His head and his hairs were white like wool, as white as snow; and his eyes were as a flame of fire; And his feet like unto fine brass, as if they burned in a furnace; and his voice as the sound of many waters." -Revelations 1:13-17

In the Book of Lamentations, it states:

"Their visage is blacker than a coal; they are not known in the streets: their skin cleaveth to their bones; it is withered, it is become like a stick." -Lamentations 4:8

"our skin was black like an oven because of the terrible famine" -Lamentations 5:10

Now Jesus, a descendant of Abraham and David, was Black, according to **Matthew 1:6**. In **Matthew 2:13-14**, it is reported that Joseph had a dream to take Mary and Jesus into Egypt because the Romans were pursuing them. If Joseph and his family were white, they would have been easily noticed in Egypt, as Shadrock Porter said in his 1992 speech at Harbour Front[1], **"God would not send his black son into a white Egypt to hide."** He sent him there to blend in with the Black inhabitants.

It should not and does not matter what colour the truth is; however, with the same breath, it is essential to acknowledge the foundation of this truth. The foundation included the earth and man was moulded from the richness of the soil. We could undoubtedly go in-depth and examine the characteristics of the Israelites and find all sorts of correlations that will confirm their identity; however, the intent here is not to prove their identity but to provide foundational information.

Throughout this book, you will be provided with undeniable evidence that depicts the Children of Israel's identity. You will see that when they left their native homeland of Israel and settled in Europe, namely the Iberian Peninsula, that they were Black. You will discover the betrayal that took place in their adopted homeland, by people that looked like them. You will also see how their Israelite identity correlated with the biblical prophecy that landed them in slavery in the Americas.

The terms *African American, African Canadian, West Indian, African, Blacks, Negros*, etc. are not terms that accurately identify the Children of Israel today. As a result, throughout

---

[1] (Identity and Power, 1992) Harbour Front Speech, Identity and Power

this book, the terms *Children of Israel*, *Children of Slaves* or *Jacobites* will be used. Why Jacobite? An Israelite is a descendant of Abraham, Isaac and Jacob, through Shem, Noah's first son. Israelites were Black, like the Hamites of Africa; however, it is essential to note that not all Black people are Israelites (not all Black people are from the line of Ham, neither are all Black people Africans).

Furthermore, an Israelite serves the God of Abraham, the God of Isaac and the God of Jacob, keeping His laws, statutes and commandments. Many of the groups that we will talk about later on refer to themselves as *Hebrew Israelites (HI)*, *Black HI*, *African HI*, and the list goes on. This is a clear indication that they are very physical and do not understand spiritual things pertaining to the KJV Bible's full teachings; they will be referred to as BHI. The term *Jacobites*, on the other hand, will be used to distinguish the descendants of the Children of slaves from all other racially identical groups.

Chapter Two

Speaking Hebrew

Many people, groups and segments of today's societies frivolously lay claim to speak the Hebrew language. There are also many documentations, books and schools that attempt to apply a historical foundation to the Hebrew language to make what has been constructed appear legitimate. However, I would argue these claims require further examination; there is still mass confusion and many questions around the Hebrew language.

The first point is there are so many references that state that today's Hebrew is not the same as the biblical Hebrew, and anyone with half a mind can refer to the popular online reference portal known as 'Wikipedia' and consider these claims and statements.

Secondly, there are many adjectives, including *extinct*, *dead*, *revival*, etc., which are used to describe the Hebrew language phenomena. However, most of these adjectives are formulated on a hypothesis surrounding such a language. Nevertheless, a simple word count in the KJV Bible reveals nothing relating to the Hebrew language per-se, yet there are references to other languages.

The third point is the claim that one needs to speak Hebrew. And to a more extreme extent, names are changed in the KJV Bible to accommodate the supposedly accurate translation of that name, which is ad hoc and inconsistent, at best. For instance, the letter 'J' is substituted for 'Y'; yet this does not apply to all words and only some names. I am not saying that this is not an accurate anthropological claim, I am merely stating that these letters are applied inconsistently by many of those who claim to use them.

If Hebrew is a modern language, and we can definitely assume that it is, then the ancient language cannot be the same, and the rationale for this will be uncovered later on. Furthermore, Hebrew would have to exist as a language for it to have died. Therefore, it cannot be revived.

On the street corners of New York, London, Toronto, and several cities around the western hemisphere, are young men, predominantly descendants of the children of slavery, shouting hateful slurs and spewing conflicting views from the scriptures. Many of them refer to themselves as *Hebrew Israelites*, *Black Hebrew Israelites*, *African Hebrew Israelites*, and various names using similar pronouns.

For the sake of consistency, they will be referred to as Black Hebrew Israelites (BHI). Most of them are members of organisations that believe they should be and are speaking Hebrew. Most claim hatred for the 'white man', incorrectly referring to him as Esau. Many have immense hatred for the 'Ashkenazi Jews' yet hold firm to his modern-day Israeli Hebrew language invention, fringes and headdresses. In general, BHI will use many antiquated phrases and the Israeli Hebrew phrases to confer a sense of authenticity to their speech.

Since it is the Israelite Nation mandate to teach all nations (**Matthew 28:16-20**), it is necessary to set the record straight. The INWWM only use the KJV version of the Bible because other versions are filled with misrepresented words and context. The God of Israel is not a God of confusion. King James I authorised the KJV Bible translation in 1611. A few years later, in 1619, the first slave ship landed on the shores of Virginia, in the Americas, carrying some twenty slaves. How is it then that the children of slavery ended up speaking in the same language as the language written in the KJV Bible? It was Porter that posed this intriguing question.

Another interesting point is why were the slaves not allowed to read the Bible, especially if they were considered stupid and less than human? There should never have been a fear in this respect. Furthermore, where did the negro spirituals come from, and why did the slaves not sing about Jesus, Peter, Paul, John, etc.?

The point is, many people are beginning to understand that the Children of Slavery and their descendants are the Children of Israel, the God of Israel being our God ensured his Children would one day read about their Forefathers. They would learn about their history and identity by reading their history book, an ingenious plan, established by the God of Israel. The INWWM does not speak nor encourage its members to speak what is today called the *Hebrew language*. Any reference to the modern-day Hebrew language will hereafter be referred to as *Israeli Hebrew*.

There is no such thing as the Hebrew Language

The first time the word Hebrew is mentioned in the KJV Bible is in **Genesis 14:13**, where Abraham is identified as a *Hebrew*. In **Exodus 2:6**, Moses is recognised as one of the *Hebrews,* and throughout the KJV Bible, the Children of Israel are often identified as *Hebrews*. Therefore, it can be argued a *Hebrew* is anyone who is descended from Abraham. Porter makes an excellent point: Jacob was the last Hebrew because the God of Israel Himself changed Jacob's name to Israel.

The language used by the descendants of The Children of Israel was referred to as the **"Language of Canaan"** in **Isaiah 19:18**, which is probably concerning the language of the time, and the **"Language of Judah"** found in **II Kings 18:28, Isaiah 36:11 and 13, Nehemiah 13:24** and **II Chronicles 32:18**.

After King David's time, the Israelite Nation was split into two kingdoms, Israel in the north and Judah in the south. The northern Kingdom of Israel was taken into captivity by the Assyrians around 740 BCE. And the Babylonians took the southern Kingdom of Judah into captivity about 570 BCE.

During their captivity in Babylon, the Israelites eventually abandoned their language (the language of Canaan) while adopting the Aramaic language, the language of their captors in Babylon. Many scholars suggest Hebrew was spoken in temples and synagogues throughout the ages and that the early bibles were translated from Hebrew, Aramaic and Greek. However, if this was fact, then there would hardly be a need for a new or modern-day Hebrew language, since Aramaic and Greek still exist in their native form, with variations to bring them to a more modern vernacular.

Language and tongue are often used interchangeably, that is why it is essential to put them in their proper context when using them. Any historical reference to the Hebrew language is based on speculation as there is no empirical data to show that the ancient Israelites spoke a language called *Hebrew*. If there was such a language called *Hebrew*, then it was a language based solely on the communication between the Israelites and their God. Therefore, as mentioned before, there is no such thing as the *Hebrew language* in the KJV bible.

Language in Context

The first mention of the term *language* was in **Genesis 11:1**. **"And the whole earth was of one language, and of one speech."**

"And the LORD said, Behold, the people is one, and they have all one language; and this they begin to do: and now nothing will be restrained from them, which they have imagined to do.7. Go to, let us go down, and there confound their language, that they may not understand one another's speech." -Genesis 11:6-7

"Therefore is the name of it called Babel; because the LORD did there confound the language of all the earth: and from thence did the LORD scatter them abroad upon the face of all the earth."
-Genesis 11:9

"Then said Eliakim, the son of Hilkiah, and Shebna, and Joah, unto Rabshakeh, Speak, I pray thee, to thy servants in the Syrian language; for we understand it: and talk not with us in the Jews' language in the ears of the people that are on the wall."
-2 Kings 18:26

The Assyrian had a language which was Syrian, so what was the Jews' language? It was not Jewish nor Hebrew, for that matter. Regardless of what it was, this statement is an apparent attempt to understand language and shows a clear distinction between what the Syrian spoke and what the Jew spoke, which is akin to English in relation to Spanish.

When the term *language* is used, it is about a people or nations, or what we call today *native language* or *native tongue*. I repeat: These are attributes for modern-day usage of the words' language and vocabulary. For instance, Spanish, Greek, Syrian and English. It was the people's language that was confounded that they may not understand one another's speech, found in **Genesis 11:1-9**. As stated previously, the so-called *Hebrew language* commonly referenced today is mainly a derivative of Yiddish, Germanic, Slavic and Romance languages. The Israelites often spoke the language familiar to the land in which they resided in.

Moses would have been considered a Hebrew, but he spoke whatever language the Egyptians spoke. Hebrew back then was a class of people, and there are many speculations as to where this came from, however, whatever the reason, the children of Israel were sometimes referred to as Hebrews, not *Hebrew Israelites*.

Moses gave us the books of the law, which are the first five books of the Bible. Many scholars claim that these books and the remaining books of the old testament, were written in Hebrew. While, others say an earlier version of Aramaic. *Hebrew* and *Aramaic* are terms that are used interchangeably when discussing the language of the Bible.

Nevertheless, Hebrew (the language) was never referred to by name, merely implicitly, like the *language of the Jews*. As the story goes, Moses was born around the 14th century BCE. In the 13th century BCE, he delivered the Children of Israel to freedom from Egyptian slavery. During this 'Exodus', he received his revelation from the God of Israel on Mount Sinai.

There is a desperate attempt to show that the Hebrew language existed. Around 2008, there was an alleged breakthrough in the Hebrew scriptures' research, which shed new light on how the Bible was written. Gershon Galil of the Department of Biblical Studies, at the University of Haifa, deciphered an inscription on a pottery shard, discovered in the Elah valley, dating from the 10th century BCE (the period of King David's reign). He claimed it was a Hebrew inscription.[2] This dubious claim really pushes the boundaries because there is no empirical data to substantiate that claim, and according to one

---

2 (EurekAlert, 2010)

professor, "the differentiation between the scripts, and between the languages themselves in that period, remains unclear."[3]

Apparently, the discovery represents the earliest known Hebrew writing. Also, the Dead Sea Scrolls were conveniently discovered in 1946/47–1956, around the same time Israel was established as a nation-state[4]. Some sources claim they were written in Aramaic and Ancient Hebrew. There was a great deal of academic controversy over the scrolls' publication because it took many decades to be published. Eventually, a Facsimile Edition of the Dead Sea Scrolls was published in 1991.

The description of Hebrew is all wrong. First, it is said, Hebrew belongs to the Northwest Semitic branch of the Afroasiatic[5] language family, yet it also carries the description of the only Canaanite language still spoken. Furthermore, this language group includes Phoenician, another non-Semitic people of whom their language is named after.

If it is Canaanite, it cannot be Semitic, because according to **Genesis 9:18**, Noah's son, Ham, is the father of Canaan. Thus, Canaan is a Hamite resulting in a Hamite language. Also, Hebrew is said to be the only truly successful example of a revived dead language. However, it could not die if it did not exist in the first place. Finally, it is said to be a language still spoken. The other is Aramaic. This is highly impossible since the vernacular is entirely different from what it would have been if it were an actual language.

The Hebrew today, which we refer to as *Israeli Hebrew*, is primarily from Yiddish, a Germanic language family. We can rightly refer to this as a *Japhetite* language family, if such a term should exist. Yiddish still thrives today, and you can even study it formally. Ladino, or Judaeo-Spanish, was Spanish spoken by Sephardic Jews. These days, most of the Ladino speakers are elderly, and most live in Israel. Their children usually either do not speak it or speak Spanish. Judaeo-Arabic was a Palestinian/Syrian/Iraqi Arabic influenced by Israelites.

It was even written in a slightly modified script. This language is endangered, with some variants extinct. Another bizarre concept was that "Hebrew ceased to be an everyday spoken language,"[6] somewhere between 200 and 400 CE. It apparently survived as the language of Jewish liturgy, rabbinic literature, intra-Jewish commerce and poetry. One

---

3 (HaaretzAP, 2008)

4 (Wikipedia, Israel, 2009)

5 (Wikipedia, Hebrew Language, 2020)

6 (Dalby, 2015) p245

could only wonder how commerce and poetry were possible if the language was no longer being *spoken*.

Hebrew Tongue

Conversely, in the biblical context, the "Hebrew tongue" mentioned in the KJV Bible, implies a way of speaking. For instance, one may have a "flattering tongue", "healing tongue", a "lying tongue", "deceitful", "false", "froward", "wholesome", "naughty", "perverse", "soft", "backbiting", "stammering", "proper", "cloven", and "unknown tongue" (all variations referenced in the KJV bible). The *Hebrew tongue* is used in these contexts, according to the KJV bible. In **Ezra 4:7,** there was a reference to the Syrian tongue; a letter was written and interpreted in the Syrian tongue. The *Greek tongue* was mentioned in **Revelations 9:11**, denoting the worship of a fallen angel by the Greeks; the name was provided in the Hebrew tongue, which was probably Aramaic.

One more point, in the Book of Acts, during the time of Pentecost, the context of the word *tongue* was clearly defined for its use at that time, in **Acts 2:8** it reads: **"And how hear we every man in our own tongue, wherein we were born?"** And in **Acts 2:11** it reads: **"Cretes and Arabians, we do hear them speak in our tongues, the wonderful works of God."**

These verses clearly show that everyone spoke in their native language and was understood by everyone else. Here, the Spirit was working as a universal translator.

Israeli Hebrew Language

The Hebrew spoken today is not the same as that which was spoken by Jesus the Christ, Moses, Daniel, King David or Abraham. Jesus the Christ spoke Aramaic, and Abraham would have spoken a form of Akkadian, Babylonia's and Chaldea's language. The modern-day Hebrew language comes from Yiddish, the historical language of the Ashke-*nazi* people who came from Eastern and Central Europe.[7]

The language is German-based, fused with elements taken from the Romance Language group and Slavic languages spoken by people from Russia, Ukraine, Poland, etc. The Sephardic Jews, comparatively, are from the Mediterranean Sea areas, including Portugal, Spain, the Middle East and Northern Africa, and make up less than 20% of what is known as the modern-day Jews. Thus, the modern version of Hebrew is not even close to the

---

7 (Kaplan, 2014)

language of our Israelite forefathers. It is redundant to learn another language to understand or study scriptures.

It is essential to note that the Bible translators were extremely careful not to use the term *Hebrew language*. Instead, they used *the Hebrew tongue*, when referring to the language spoken by our Israelite forefathers, who were sometimes called Hebrews by strangers, not knowing that Jacob was surnamed *Israel*.

However, our forefathers, Abraham, Isaac and Jacob, were called *Hebrews*. Still, it is careless for strangers to assume that these men spoke the Hebrew language since there is no such reference in the Bible. For example, Abraham was Chaldean, and since he never heard of a Hebrew language, would have spoken a Babylonian language, Akkadian. Likewise, as stated earlier, Jesus the Christ spoke Aramaic, Moses spoke Egyptian, etc.

According to numerous texts, namely the Eerdmans Bible Dictionary, "Él"[8,] is singular for *god* and "Elohim"[9] is plural, meaning *gods*. The Ugarit text (c. 1200 BCE), and other Canaanite sources, suggests the high god of the Canaanite pantheon was El, whose wife, the mother of the gods, was Asherah. El is also the father of the lesser gods, known as the *children of El*; these include Baal, Anat, Astarte, Dagan, Moloch, etc. A list of these deities can be found on 'Wikipedia', under "Ancient Canaanite religion." El and Elohim also appear to be titles like *Mr, Dr* etc. It should be noted "'Ilāh"[10] in Arabic means "deity" or "god" and is linguistically related to El, which is to say, another title. That means Allāh, I would argue, is the name of *a* god.

Yahweh (Yahveh) appears to be related to the term *"I AM Who I AM"*. The name *Yahweh* occurs on the Moabite stone and appears as a divine name in various ancient texts.[11] According to the 'Britannica Encyclopedia'[12], Latin-speaking scholars substituted the 'Y' (which does not exist in Latin) with 'I' or 'J' (the latter of which exists in Latin as a variant form of 'I'). With so much misperception to Yahweh's origin and meaning, somehow El/Elohim merged into Yahweh[13], and Elohim and Yahweh are used interchangeably

---

8 (Myers, 1987) p316

9 Ibid p331

10 (Wikipedia, Ilah, 2020)

11 (Myers, 1987) p1075

12 (Mahajan, 2008)

13 (Wikipedia, Yahweh, 2020) El and Yahweh became conflated and El-linked epithets such as El Shaddai came to be applied to Yahweh alone.

among the Modern Hebrew speakers, BHIs, Ashkenazi Jews and some Christians. Also, when you become a 3rd degree Mason, you learn:

"The true name of Satan, the Kabalists say, is Yahveh reversed; for Satan is not a black god, but the negation of God."[14]

Yahveh is Yahweh, and according to Albert Pike in his infamous book "Morals and Dogma", *Yahweh* reversed is Satan's actual name. He also points out that Satan is not a Black god that insinuates what we as Israelites know, that the God of Israel is Black. It would be better to stay away from these so-called Hebrew terms for God with all the confusion.

At best, *El*, *Elohim* and their current variation, *Yahweh*, are merely titles associated with the word 'god'. The worst-case scenario, given by Albert Pike, is that Yahweh is Satan's actual name. Now, the term 'God', in the English vernacular, on the other hand, is the universal title given to a supreme being. Understanding that God is a title is imperative and something understood by our forefathers. Even the God of Israel understood the importance of a name, that contrasts with what the masses understand today. It seems that scholars and blind followers are all concerned with a title because they do not know God's name.

"The Teachers, even of Christianity, are, in general, the most ignorant of the true meaning of that which they teach. There is no book of which so little is known as the Bible. To most who read it, it is as incomprehensible as the Sohar."[15]

Furthermore, in an article "The Christian Invention of Judaism" by Daniel Boyarin, he argues that the *development* of Christian orthodoxy involved the production of Christian *heresies* and hailed the existence of another *orthodoxy*, that being Judaism. Judaism is thus the 'dark double' of Christianity, the so-called "true-religion" (orthodoxy or Ekklesia), "in order for there to be a true Ekklesia, there had to be a false one too."[16]

In summary, Boyarin's article appears to inadvertently suggest Christianity, or the Christian philosophy, was invented, created, or as in the term above developed over time, Judaism was created as its opposite. Ignatius of Antioch wanted to create a definitive boundary between the Jews and Christians and thus inadvertently created the two opposing forces. Nevertheless, they are more complementary than opposing.

---

[14] (Pike, 1871) p102

[15] (Pike, 1871) pdf version p95

[16] (Boyarin, 2016)

The point here is, out of one of these newly invented philosophies, came the Israeli Hebrew Language. The hidden secret is that creating a new concept called Judaism gave birth to a new language. It is structured around a completely different people with a different culture, philosophy and god. It has no bases for the Children of Israel, the Israelite way of life or the God of Israel.

The Name of God

It is imperative to note that the God of Israel has many names. For instance, in **Exodus 6:3**, he tells Moses, **"[...] I appeared unto Abraham, unto Isaac, and unto Jacob, by the name of God Almighty, but by my name JEHOVAH was I not known to them."**

When the God of Israel revealed Himself to Moses, in preparation for bringing His people out of Egypt, He instructed Moses to refer to Him as the **"the God of Abraham, the God of Isaac, and the God of Jacob,"** in **Exodus 3:15**, stating that this is His name forever. He also instructed Moses to identify Him by that name when speaking to the Children of Israel, in verse 16. Here, the name carries a few important implications:

1. When God identified Himself as the God of Abraham, Isaac, and Jacob, He clearly distinguished Himself from any other gods, especially the gods of Egypt in whose land the Israelites dwelt. In addition to this, He did not give permission to use His other names.
2. The reference to Abraham, Isaac, and Jacob implies this is the same God that the Israelites' forefathers worshipped.
3. The God of Israel's name speaks to the covenant made with three different generations, Abraham, Isaac, and Jacob, and the blessings and promises emphasised in the covenant.

The God of Israel first calls Abram out of Ur of the Chaldees to the land of Canaan, establishing a covenant with him, in **Genesis 12:1–3**, and changed his name to Abraham. He reaffirms the same covenant with Abraham's son, Isaac, in **Genesis 21:12; 26:3–4,** and later with Isaac's son, Jacob, in **Genesis 28:14–15**. The God who established and sanctioned this covenant is rightly called *the God of Abraham, the God of Isaac, and the God of Jacob*. This name of God emphasises the covenant that He made with Israel and the Israelites.

This name is used throughout the scriptures, and even Jesus the Christ used this name to teach a lesson on the resurrection to the Sadducees:

"About the resurrection of the dead—have you not read what God said to you, 'I am the God of Abraham, the God of Isaac, and the God of Jacob'? He is not the God of the dead but of the living" -Matthew 22:31–32

In **Acts 3**, when Peter preaches to the Israelites in the temple, he refers to *the God of Abraham, Isaac and Jacob*, a name that his brethren would have commonly used in their worship. Peter and John had just healed a lame man, who was now standing before them. Peter attributes the miracle to the power of the God of Abraham, Isaac and Jacob, working through Jesus. In other words, Peter was careful to link the miracle they had just witnessed to the one and only God of their fathers. The same God who spoke to the patriarchs was at work in their midst.

In explaining the miracle of a lame man walking, Peter also sets up a bold contrast:

"The God of Abraham, Isaac and Jacob, the God of our fathers, has glorified his servant Jesus. You handed him over to be killed, and you disowned him before Pilate" -Acts 3:13.

The God whom the Jews purported to revere treated Jesus of Nazareth much differently than they had: God glorified Jesus and killed Him. Peter hammers home the contrast in verse 15: **"You killed the author of life, but God raised him from the dead."** In closing, Peter reminds his audience that the God of Abraham, Isaac, and Jacob was fulfilling His covenant with them in verse 25: **"You are heirs of the prophets and of the covenant God made with your fathers."**

The Invention of EBY

The Hebrew status shift to a full-fledged native language is most commonly referred to as the "revival" of Hebrew. However, while not used as an everyday all-purpose vernacular, pre-twentieth century Hebrew cannot be regarded as a dead language.

"Its most unusual feature was not it was 'dead' (a much-abused term) and had to be 'artificially revived', but that it was no one's mother tongue, and that there were no speakers of any dialects closely related to it."[17]

The "Jewish" population in Palestine in the nineteenth century included mainly the Sephardi communities and the Ashkenazi communities. The Sephardi communities spoke either Judeo-Spanish, or Judeo-Arabic and Arabic. The Ashkenazi communities, for the most part, had Yiddish as their vernacular.[18]

---

[17] (Blanc, 1968) p237

[18] See Eliav 1978: 156 with n100; also, as well as for other small organisations, Parfitt 1972: 241-2.

Eliezer Ben-Yehuda[19], later known as "the father of the Hebrew language revival," vigorously raised the call for reviving the Hebrew language as a prerequisite for this Jewish national revival. He fought passionately for its spread as a spoken language, even so far as to make his eldest son (born in 1882) speak Hebrew as his first language. Nevertheless, it was not until the beginning of the twentieth century, after the arrival of another wave of immigration (the so-called *"Second Aliya"*), that the rapid spread of spoken Hebrew and the nativisation of Hebrew took place. From 1916-18, more than 75% of the young population in the new settlements in Palestine used Hebrew as their sole or primary language, and numbers of native speakers of Hebrew steadily grew.[20]

By 1921, Modern Hebrew became an official language in British-ruled Palestine (along with English and Arabic). Finally, in 1948 Modern Hebrew was proclaimed the official language of the newly declared State of Israel. This language combines many of the previously spoken languages of Ladino, Arabic, Latin, Persian and Aramaic, with heavy influence from Yiddish, Russian and German. Many new words were either borrowed from or coined after European languages, especially English, Yiddish, Russian, and German.

Today, most self-proclaimed Hebrew speakers speak EBY whether they know it or not. EBY is the term coined by Elder Andil Holder during one of his online presentations. EBY is the Israeli Hebrew we have been utilising within this text.

It is not disrespectful, but pure fact, that we refer to the term 'invention' rather than 'revival'. In practice, Israeli Hebrew is widely used in Ashkenazi Jewish services and studies in Israel and abroad. The Yiddish influenced it. The following are some interesting facts about Eliezer Ben-Yehuda.

1. He was born Eliezer Yitzhak Perelman in Lithuania but later changed his name to Eliezer Ben-Yehuda. Changing names is a practice that most Israeli Hebrew speakers, including the HBI, seem to have adopted.
2. He left Russia in 1878 to study medicine in Paris.
3. He arrived in Palestine in 1881, at the beginning of the waves of Jewish (Khazar) immigration to come, having already published several articles on renewing the Jewish people, their land and language.
4. He coined new Hebrew words for everyday objects like dolls, jelly, towels, bicycles.

---

[19] (Fellman, 2020)

[20] (Izre'el, n.d.)

5.   He became involved in the first efforts in Palestine to use Hebrew as the standard language in school, despite the shortage of textbooks, materials, games, songs, vocabulary and teachers who could follow his example.

6.   He became a lexicographer to encourage the Hebrew language's adoption while describing vocabulary according to rigorously philological lines. Including **eliminating Aramaic** and other foreign words from ancient texts–though he did introduce transliterations from modern tongues.

7.   This contributed to his full Ancient and Modern Hebrew dictionary. He worked on it day and night, publishing six volumes in his lifetime. After his death, his wife and son continued to publish his manuscript, completing the seventeenth and last volume in 1959.

8.   In 1890, he founded the "Hebrew Language Council" to arbitrate matters of terminology, pronunciation, spelling and punctuation for Hebrew use.

9.   Russian influence is particularly evident in Hebrew. For example, the Russian suffix '-acia' is used in nouns, where English has the suffix '-ation'.

10.   In November 1922, the British mandate authorities recognised Hebrew as the official language of the Jews of Palestine. A month later, Eliezer Ben-Yehuda died.

With the rise of Zionism in the 19th century, Israeli Hebrew was developed as a spoken and literary language, becoming the primary language of the Yishuv and subsequently of the State of Israel. According to Ethnologue, in 1998, Israeli Hebrew was the language of five million people worldwide. After Israel, the United States has the second-largest Israeli Hebrew-speaking population, with about 220,000 fluent speakers, mostly Israeli.[21]

Spirit to Spirit

Secretly, our Israelite forefathers were known to utilise a spiritual or holy tongue. This so-called *language of the Holy Sanctuary*, as it was commonly known, was never a literary language. There was no alphabet, so nothing was written. It was an unknown tongue spoken on occasions Spirit to Spirit; i.e. between the God of Israel and His chosen, or His representative, or ONE selected member of his Israelite Royal Family.

It was an unusual and unique state of spiritual communication and not for typical everyday use. The God of Israel is the most excellent teacher, which is recognised in His communication and education method. The God of Israel has never attempted to communicate using a foreign tongue like the Israeli Hebrew language, aka Yiddish.

"And he said unto me, Son of man, go, get thee unto the house of Israel, and speak with my words unto them. For thou art not sent to a people of a strange speech and of an hard language, but to the house of Israel." -Ezekiel 3:4-6;4

---

[21] (Wikipedia, Hebrew Language, 2020)

"Whom shall he teach knowledge? And whom shall he make to understand doctrine? Them that are weaned from the milk, and drawn from the breasts. For precept must be upon precept, precept upon precept; line upon line, line upon line; here a little, and there a little: For with stammering lips and another tongue will he speak to this people." -Isaiah 28: 9-11 9

Instead, the God of Israel communicated to his people, the Israelites, in the language they spoke their *native tongue*. Therefore, those who desire to speak an unknown tongue glorify not the God of Israel, but the Spirit of the Air, so there would be no enlightenment for the Israelite Nation, as written in **1 Corinthians 14:1-9.** The KJV Bible was translated into English because English is the dominant language of the children of slavery.

In **Acts 22**, we read of Saul, whose name was changed to Paul, who once persecuted his brethren. Now he had to face his brethren after being transformed spiritually. Do you not suppose he was always able to speak their language? Paul was a well-educated man, who was around them all the time, communicating with them and persecuting them, while having their blood flow through his veins. He even tells us that he is an Israelite, of the seed of Abraham, of the tribe of Benjamin (see **Romans 11**). Paul could speak with his brethren differently for the first time. Paul was always able to speak their language (the two dominant languages being Aramaic and Greek). Still, he never spoke the *Hebrew tongue* until that time because the tongue suggests a way of speaking, which carries a higher level of spiritual insight.

In the Bible, we often see Israelites singing songs after miracles, battles, and various reasons. Songs were used to pass on messages for generations. Here are a few examples from the scriptures:
- **Exodus 15:1** - Moses sang after Pharaoh was drowned.
- **Numbers 21:17** - Israel sang after hearing they received water.
- **Deuteronomy 31:19** - God told Moses to write a song as a witness against Israel.
- **2 Samuel 22:1** - David sang when he was delivered from his enemies.
- **Psalms 30:1** - A song of dedication at the house of David.

The Jacobites have always been musical people. The more we learn about our history, the more we see that there is a very real effort to hide the truth. Finally, could you possibly imagine the poor old children of slavery having to speak Hebrew to glorify the God of Israel?

Their pain and emotions were raw, yet they sang songs about Abraham, Joseph and Moses. They sang, in English, songs of hope and faith and about God and conveyed their emotions Spiritually and effectively. Their songs showed the connection the Children of Slavery had with the Children of Israel in the scripture, and their similar plight, oppression and Canaan land. They sang to tell their stories and remember what the God of Israel did for their forefathers.

They sang for Moses, their deliverer, and for Pharaoh to be dealt with; they sang out their battle cries and their victories. These slave songs would become notoriously known as Negro spirituals or songs of the *Negro's Spirit*. And as they rose against their enemies and were struck down by the oppressors, they did so vehemently believe that they were the children of the Almighty God of Israel—in all of this and in their desperation, they did not speak the Israeli Hebrew language.

Conclusion

In conclusion, I have proved using scriptures that there is no such thing as the Hebrew language during biblical times. I have also investigated the composition of the Israeli Hebrew Language used today and have argued the rationale for the Hebrew tongue, as it pertains to a specific context in the KJV Bible, implying a way of speaking.

We should understand why we do not speak the Hebrew language and why it is unnecessary to learn a new made-up language to understand the KJV Bible's scriptures. However, many people believe this is necessary, and that is their choice. While there is a debate as to how often Hebrew was used, 'Britannica' tells us that the first form of Hebrew was not used among the people as a spoken language.

We cannot find the phrase *Hebrew language* in the KJV bible. When the children of Israel were in captivity in Egypt, they eventually spoke Egyptian and likewise, when they were in Babylon, they spoke whatever it was that the Babylonians spoke. Now that we are in the Americas, we talk about a dialect of the English language. The dominant language often prevails. To say something is not the same as proving it. We are told that Ugaritic, Phoenician, Aramaic, Syriac, Arabic and Canaanite are Semitic languages. However, that does not make sense, since Phoenicians and Canaanites were descendants of Ham.

The code to unlock the translation of the KJV Bible was not given to the translators because their job was not to understand, but to translate. That is why they have used several previous translations, and this is also why Hebrew is misconstrued.

The Hebrew tongue is a spiritual expression, and this is demonstrated from Babel to Pentecost; there is the scattering and a gathering through the Spirit of the language. The Hebrew tongue is not a physical expression of letters, vowels and consonants, rather a communication (edification) from Spirit to Spirit. The person who is speaking is connected to other Israelites and people who understand what is being said. They are all under the umbrella of one Spirit from the God of Israel.

In 2020, the INWWM online broadcasts received many messages stating that they have never heard teachings like that. The doctrine we have sounded different from regular preaching. Yet, we speak in English to a predominantly English-speaking audience—could this be the true essence of the Hebrew tongue, as described in Acts, regarding the day of Pentecost?

Chapter Three

Historical Identity

After King Solomon's death around 930 BCE, the kingdom of Israel was divided due to internal conflict. There was Israel to the North and Judah to the south. In addition to the internal battles, Israel and Judah were taken into captivity at various times over the next few hundred years. Furthermore, the inhabitants fled Israel settling in other countries.

One of the first invasions was by the Assyrian king, Sargon II, in 720 BCE. According to King Sargon's inscriptions,

"27,290 Jews were deported from Israel and resettled across the Assyrian Empire, following the standard Assyrian way of dealing with defeated enemy peoples through resettlement."[22]

Another invasion was led by the Assyrian king, Sennacherib, in approximately 701 BCE. He attacked the fortified cities of the Kingdom of Judah in a campaign of subjugation. However, even though Sennacherib besieged Jerusalem, he failed to capture it.

Then in 597 BCE, the Babylonian king, Nebuchadnezzar II, attacked and laid siege on Jerusalem. Following the siege of 597 BC, Nebuchadnezzar installed King Zedekiah as a vassal king of Judah at 21. However, Zedekiah revolted against Babylon and entered an alliance with Pharaoh Hophra, the king of Egypt. Nebuchadnezzar responded by invading Judea, found in **2 Kings 25:1**.

The Greek King, Antiochus IV Epiphanes, persecuted the Israelites in Judea and Samaria, sparking the Maccabean insurrection in 168 BCE. In 63 CE, another siege of Jerusalem took place during Pompey the Great's campaigns in the East. His conquest of Jerusalem

---

[22] (wikipedia, 2020)

marked the end of Israelite independence. Jerusalem was incorporated as a client kingdom of the Roman Republic.

In August 70 CE, the Romans, led by General Titus, besieged Jerusalem, breached the city's final defences and massacred most of the remaining population.[23] It was at this time, when the Romans destroyed much of the city, including the Second Temple. Nearly all Israelites were driven to seek refuge throughout the Mediterranean lands, including Egypt, Northern Africa, Turkey and even south India, where remnants of their existence still stand today.

Those in Italy, Greece and Turkey refused to worship the Gods of the Roman Empire and thus had to flee, migrating to North African countries. Some Israelites also went to South Sudan, Uganda and Yemen. It is important ////to note that Israel, the land, never regained its footing and have been subjected to insurrections and wars. The land Israel took on several names as it became part of the Roman/Byzantine empire, from *Palaestina* to *Palestine*.

The 7th century CE gave birth to Islam, and most of the coastal cities of North Africa were under Muslim rule as they executed their dictum, 'convert or die'. By 790 CE, the Israelite Empire of Ghana was known world-wide. Ghana was called "The Land of Gold," and there was no wealthier Empire anywhere to be found. However, in 1076, the Mahommedans, or a Muslim sect called the Almoravids, attacked Ghana with devastating results. It must be stressed that these Muslims were Black people (usually native African converts), differing mainly in appearance from the Israelites by the earrings and turban they wore.

"They ruthlessly imposed their Islamic cult on the Israelite elites, ravaged the Empire and imposed heavy taxes. Western Africa would never be the same again. Attempts to rebuild were quite successful in Mali and Songhai, but the evil presence of the Mahommedans refused to go away. In 1591, they attacked again, and the lights over Western Africa went out permanently. Now it was time to unleash the second force of evil."[24]

The Iberian Peninsula

Israelites who could not flee to other parts of Africa, simply converted to Islam. One such Israelite was Tariq ibn Ziad, for whom the Rock of Gibraltar (Jabal Tariq) was named. In 711, as Governor of Mauritania, he led an invasion of mainly Israelites into the Iberian

---

23 (Lohnes, 2018)

24 (Hinds & Castrilli, 1995, December 29) p86

Peninsula (Spain and Portugal), defeating King Roderic. This invasion was known as the Muslim Umayyad conquest of Visigothic Hispania. For the next 780 years, the Moors (Israelites and Muslims) ruled in the Iberian Peninsula. The Muslims dominated the political scene, and the Israelites laid the foundation for European civilisation.

"Between 900 and 1300 A.D., Spain became the most educationally advanced country in the world, as the Israelites led the field in science, astronomy, mathematics, finance, philosophy, mysticism, literature, religion, medicine and geography. All the nations of Europe came to Spain to drink of Israelite knowledge."[25]

By the 15th Century, the Muslim power structure was weakening due to internal strife, resulting in the Europeans' assertion of power. The Spanish Inquisition was eventually established in 1478 by Catholic Monarchs Ferdinand II of Aragon and Isabella I of Castile. The Inquisition came with great persecution as it promoted the Christian philosophy adopting the Muslims' "convert or die" slogan.

"Many Jews also are scattered over this region some natives boasting themselves of Abraham's seed inhabiting both sides of the river Niger: Others are Asian strangers who fled thither either from the desolation of Jerusalem by Vespasian; or from Judea wasted and depopulated years Romans, Persians, Saracens, and Christians: Or else such as came out of Europe, whence they were banished, out of some parts of Italy in the year 1342. out of Spain in the year 1462. out of the lower countries in 1350. out of France in 1403. out of England in 1422. These all differ in hanit, and are divided into several tribes, having no dominion, though both wealthy and numerous, but despised of all nations, and so abominated by the Turks that they are not admitted to be Mahumetans unless first baptised: and the no otherwise made use of than to receive their customs and gather their taxes."[26]

In 1492 and 1502 royal decrees were issued ordering Muslims and Jews [Israelites] to convert to Catholicism or leave Castile, furthering the prophecy of **Deuteronomy 28:64**,

"And the LORD shall scatter thee among all people, from the one end of the earth even unto the other; and there thou shalt serve other gods, which neither thou nor thy fathers have known, even wood and stone."

---

[25] (Hinds & Castrilli, 1995, December 29) p79

[26] (Ogilby, 1670) p34

Israelites that did not convert were now forcefully deported to Northern or Western Africa while others fled to Portugal.

"The official chronicler of king Joao II (1481 - 1495) Garcia D Resende, reports on one of the methods to populate this island that also throws some light on a tragic form of Jewish participation in the Portuguese Atlantic empire. The king had allowed Jewish refugees from Spain (from where they had been expelled in 1492) to remain in Portugal only in return for payment of an enormous ransom. In 1493 those who could not pay had their children taken away from them baptized by force, and deported to San Tome in order to raise to be raised as Christians and to help populate the island that the king had just leased to Alvaro de Caminha at an annual rent of 100,000 reis."[27]

Interestingly, after fleeing Spain and leaving all their wealth behind, the Portuguese King allowed the Israelites to travel through Portugal. He taxed them and local Israelites heavily for this service and gave eight months for the Spanish Israelites to leave. However, the Spanish Israelites received news of the atrocious crimes inflicted upon their brethren that had begun their journey to the African coast. It was so bad that they preferred meeting death in Portugal instead of being pillaged, raped, their clothes taken from them and being generally mistreated or even killed. Unfortunately, the time allowance expired and a plague broke out in Portugal, in which the Spanish Israelites were blamed. The King of Portugal issued an edict which was the epitome of **Deuteronomy 28:32** and extending the terror.

"All Jewish children below fourteen years of age were torn from their parents arms, dragged into the church; baptized. Those under three years of age were given to Christians, to receive a Christian education or in other words to be raised as slaves; those between three and ten years of age were put on board of a ship and conveyed to the newly discovered unwholesome island of St. Thomas called 'Ilhas Perdidas' 'the iles of perdition' [or the island of punishment] which was colonized by Portuguese condemned criminals, to fare there as best they could. Those between ten and fourteen years were sold as slaves."[28]

It got worse: "Mother's cast themselves at the feet of the tyrants and pitifully begged to be taken with their babies; they were heartlessly thrust aside. Hundreds of mothers mad

---

27

28 (Krauskopf, 1887) p213

with despair ran behind the ships as they carried off the idols of their heart and perished in the waves."[29]

Who could imagine, but this was not the end. The Israelites from Spain finally decided to leave Portugal, "but they were told that they had forfeit their right and were given the choice between baptism and slavery." [30]

Thousands of Israelites were tortured before being sold into slavery and sent to West Africa. The atrocities continued extending to the children of the Portuguese Israelites. However, in Portugal, the Christian government of King Manoel issued its decree expelling all Israelites.

According to Porter, when the Israelites were officially thrown out of Portugal, many ended up in West Africa, in countries like Niger, Sierra Leone, the Gold Coast, and Angola[31], including an island off the west coast called San Thome [St. Thomas]. These places were associated with the Portuguese. The Portuguese named many of these places like the mysterious 'Kingdom of Juda' located along the slave coast. For instance, the Kingdom of Juda, which can be found on the 1747 Bowen map, also called *whydah*, *Fida*, *Hwedah*, *Ouidah*, *Judah* or *Ajuda*, also *the Island of San Thome*, was discovered and operated by the Portuguese, similar to that of Australia, a jail.[32] The Israelites were known as *Black Portuguese* or *Black Spaniards*, *Jew* or *Black Jew*. The Israelites of Spain were referred to as *Negro*, which is Spanish for 'Black'.

"King John II in 1492 expelled all the Jews to the island of St. Thomas, which had been discovered in 1471, and to other Portuguese settlements on the continent of Africa; and from these banished Jews, the black Portuguese, as they are called, and **the Jews in Loango, who are despised even by the very Negroes**, are descended. By these colonists, St. Thomas soon became a considerable place of trade, and valuable for its sugar plantations. Thirty years after their settlement, not less than one hundred and fifty-six thousand ar-robes (of thirty pounds weight each) of sugar were exported; and the engines of sixty sugar works, turned by slaves. These Negroes were purchased in Guinea, Congo,

---

[29] Ibid 215

[30] Ibid 216

[31] (Porter E. S., The Truth, The Lie and The Bible, 1995) p 6

[32] *Ibid* p 6

and Manicongo, and the colonists had plantations furnished with from one hundred and fifty to three thousand Negro slaves."[33]

Slavery is a familiar concept that has occurred since biblical times. The mistreatment of human beings deprived of personal rights has appeared in many forms throughout the world. However, one institution stands out for its global scale and its lasting legacy: The Transatlantic slave trade. Spanning three continents (Europe, Africa and the Americas), between 1450, (1611 being the prominent date for North America) and the early 19th Century, millions of lives were traded and/or lost, enacting the infamous **Deuteronomy 28:68.**

"And the LORD shall bring thee into Egypt again with ships, by the way whereof I spake unto thee, Thou shalt see it no more again: and there ye shall be sold unto your enemies for bondmen and bondwomen, and no man shall buy you."

Looking at what we have reviewed thus far, it appears that the Israelites were being primed for the Transatlantic slave trade. They were under siege, persecuted, scattered and subjected to unspeakable cruelty from Israel to North Africa, to Europe and the Iberian Peninsula, and to West Africa. Their children were ripped away from their parents. They were taken to many Portuguese colonies along the west coast of Africa where they were baptised into the Christian philosophy and learned how to fend for themselves. Yet the trail seemed to be made of bread crumbs that have been plucked away by the scavengers of history.

The ugly inception of Christianity left many people questioning the True Israelites' identity, while giving credence to the imposters, Ashkenazi Jews. Ironically some people believe the Jacobites were Christians way before the transatlantic slave trade. However, the previous references are the empirical evidence of forced conversion. Moreover, the children would have had difficulty maintaining their culture as was intended by the forceful removal from their parents at such tender ages. Unfortunately, this is also the reason why so many Jacobites lack understanding of their identity.

Those That Call Themselves Jews

It just so happens that around 9th Century the Khazars, a Turkic people from Eastern Europe near the Caucasus mountains, converted to the "Israelite Religion." You can find out more about how this was done by reading "The Word, The Israelite and the Damned" or "The Spirit of Egypt in America" written by Elder Shadrock Porter's students. You can

---

33 (The Critical Review, Or, Annals of Literature, Volume 57 edited by Tobias Smollett, 1783)

also read the "The Thirteenth Tribe" written 1976 by Arthur Koestler.[34] He advances the thesis that Ashkenazi Jews are not descended from the historical Israelites of antiquity, but from Khazars, a Turkic people. However, to provide a brief synopsis: Khazars are the seventh son of Togarmah, Japheth's grandson and brother of Ashkenaz.

According to the KJV 1611 Bible, in **Genesis 10:2-5**, his great uncles were Gog and Magog. The Khazars/Ashkenazi was spared the Muslim onslaught, as they defeated the Arabs in 653 CE at Balanjar. Therefore, the Khazars/Ashkenazi held the balance of power between the Mahommedans and the Byzantine Christians.

These eastern European Khazars and their Ashkenazi cousins also travelled throughout Europe from Turkey, ending up in Spain and Portugal and adopted the Israelite way of life. However, instead of being persecuted alongside the Israelites, they assumed his Identity and financed the slave trade. Nevertheless, the truth always prevails and from time to time a bread crumb appears, between 1736-1748 it was written:

" **'Tis also a vulgar Error that the Jews are all black; for this is only true of the Portuguese Jews**? Who marrying always among one another, beget Children like themselves; and consequently, the Swarthiness of their Complexion is entail'd upon their whole Race, even in the Northern Regions. But the Jews who are originally of Germany; those, for example, I have seen at Prague, are not blacker than the rest of their Countrymen."[35]

This passage clearly shows that the true Israelites were Black, and the Khazars and Ashkenazi were not.

The African Connection

Some historians have hotly contested the plight of the Israelites; However, the fact remains, the Israelites were in Africa long before the Atlantic slave trade began. There are many scholarly accounts which also show the Israelites as being Black. Simultaneously, several of these scholars may have varying ideas, providing pertinent details that helped draw the correlations between the descendants of the children of slavery and the biblical Israelites.

Some books offer detailed descriptions of the Israelite customs in many African tribes. However, some of these tribes were the leading suppliers of slaves during the slave trade.

---

[34] (Koestler, 1976)

[35] (Misson, 1736-1748,)

Most Israelites in the west are descendants from those tribes. Two important factors should be made clear and will be discussed later-on:
1. Israelites were not native to the land of Africa unless one believes that the land of Israel is part of Africa.
2. It was the native Africans and Arab traders that sold the Israelites into slavery.

Nevertheless, in reading some of these narratives, it is essential to understand the context in which some of them were written, the timeframe and the author's background.

One such book is "Hebrewisms of West Africa" by Joseph J. Williams. In a detailed account, he gives evidence to show the religious and cultural similarity of ancient Israelites to the West African tribes, particularly the Ashanti. He finds parallels between the two peoples in various ways, including custom, belief, ritual, law and culture. Without jumping to conclusions, Williams finds the evidence so overwhelming that he cannot help but find that the Ashanti are the descendants of the Israelites. [36]

However, most historians such as Williams do not consider that wherever the Israelites travelled, they significantly influenced the local communities. As a result, it would appear that these communities were practising the Israelite culture because it was native, whereas these cultures could have just as easily been adopted.

Porter not only believes the Israelites travelled all over Africa, he also believes they settled and established communities. He went as far as establishing many connections and correlations between the children of slavery, who were taken in chains from the shores of West Africa and brought to the Americas, resulting in the legitimate claim that the ancient Israelites were our ancestors. Much of the slave narrative and connection is documented in his books:
1. "The Truth, The Lie and The Bible"
2. "The Word, The Israelite and the Damned"
3. "The Forgotten Israelites"
4. "The Spirit of Egypt in America"

As mentioned earlier, Israel was being primed for their final destination. They were no longer keeping the laws, statutes and commandments, and many had been forcefully converted to Christianity or Islam, their Identity was slowly ebbing away. For centuries, Europeans, Africans and Arabs were in constant contact with the Mediterranean, bridging

---

[36] Hebrewisms of West Africa; From Nile to Niger with the Jews, (N.Y.: The Dial Press, 1931), P36. 1. Joseph J. Williams, colonists,

the continents. As a result, millions of Israelites were sent to the Americas and sold into slavery.

Millions died in transit across the middle passage and were cast into the Atlantic Ocean's watery grave. Millions suffered savage treatment during their capture and while being groomed in the slave palaces. Millions experienced inhumane conditions aboard slave ships, which accompanied the brutal crushing of any resistance, torcher, battery, abuse, and the list goes on.

This atrocity affected the slaves, and their descendants, world economies and histories to this very day. The crops grown in the new territories, sugar cane, tobacco and cotton, were labour-intensive. There were not enough colonists or indentured servants to farm all the new land. Europeans enslaved American Natives; however, though some successfully fought, many died from new diseases which came with the Europeans. Consequently, to fulfil the enormous demand for labour, the Europeans were looking towards Africa.

This industry persisted in different ways for centuries. Many African tribes had slaves, and sometimes these slaves could become part of the family of a master, some were able to own property, and even ascend to a master's family or influential positions. However, when white captains came offering manufactured goods, weapons and rum for slaves, African kings, chiefs and merchants had little reason to hesitate. They viewed the people they sold not as fellow Africans but criminals, debtors, or prisoners of war from rival tribes.

One thing that history does not explain in great details is the so-called rival tribes. Many of these were Israelite communities. It is a known fact that there were Israelite communities in these regions because, for one, the Portuguese had placed some of them in those communities. The native Africans could not have been very happy or hospitable to the people now invading their lands and setting up communities; thus, the Israelites were an easy target for the slave trade.

There were also several insurrections and resistance by these Israelite communities and some of their leaders. Queen Nzinga of Angola, in 1663, led one such resistance. She was known as the unconquerable queen. It is written in Portugal's official documents (the written record used by almost all historians of Africa) that Nzinga, on her deathbed, had returned to the same Church that had baptised her as "Ann". Yet she was one of the very first to see that the Portuguese conquests, the slave trade, and the Church were all inseparably the same.

The long years of warfare, where she led her people to defend their rights, had been equally against Portuguese conquests, the slave trade and the Church. She was said to have called this union of **the unholy trinity.** She had never surrendered. In 1963, three hundred years after her death, her people, now catholic themselves, did not believe she had returned to the Church.

Ironically, Porter spoke of another Nzinga, king of the Congo kingdom, Nzinga Kuwu, who was conned into Christianity by the Portuguese in 1492. His name was changed to Joao I, as Porter suggests, this is one of the many ways the Israelites lost their Identity. Nevertheless, Africa was in chaos. Kings enriched their domains and fortified them against neighbouring rivals by selling them. The slave trade caused African kingdoms to prosper.

However, it also caused intense competition to meet the enormous European demand. Slavery replaced other criminal penalties, and capturing slaves became a motivation for war, rather than its consequence. The neighbouring kingdoms required European firearms, which they often purchased for slaves, to protect themselves from slave raids.

The ugly truth is that Europeans did not capture and enslave people themselves. Rather they bought the slaves from the native African and Muslim[37] slave traders (which many were Africans who converted to Islam), who restricted the European traders to a few points on the African coast. At the same time, they invaded the interior to provide slaves to the Europeans.[38] The European traders sold weapons to the African slave traders, but did not instigate the wars; they used the wars to enrich themselves. There were times when armies of African tribes enslaved the inhabitants of conquered Israelite towns and villages.

At other times, raiding parties kidnapped individuals or captured isolated families. As the conflicts spread to the interior, captives had to march for hundreds of miles to the coast where European traders awaited them. The African raiders and traders tied the captives together with rope or secured them with wooden yokes around their necks. It was a terrifying experience, and many captives died from exhaustion, hunger and exposure during the journey. Others killed themselves rather than submit to their fate, and the raiders killed those who resisted.

---

37 (The Critical Review, Or, Annals of Literature, Volume 57 edited by Tobias Smollett, 1783)

38 (Stern, 2007)

The slave trade became an arms race, changing the continent's cultures and currencies. The slaves themselves faced unprecedented cruelty as the spirit of greed permeated throughout the African kingdoms. The slaves were loaded into boats bound for the New Egypt (the Americas) after being marched to slave forts known as slave palaces, shaved to avoid lice, and branded on the coast. Around 20% of them never saw land again. In his 1992 speech[39] Porter points out why they were called *'Slave Palaces'* if it were not for the knowledge that they were built to hold *royalty*. The mockery is akin to the crucifixion of Jesus the Christs'– the robe, crown of thorns and the title "King of the Jews."

Insufficient hygiene forced many to die of sickness, and ship crew cast others overboard for being ill. As a disciplinary action, by cutting off the ears of slaves as evidence of purchase, the captains secured their income. Some captives took matters into their own hands. Some inland Africans had never seen whites before and believed they were cannibals, dragging away people daily and returning for more. Afraid of being eaten or to avoid further suffering, they committed suicide or starved themselves, believing that their souls would return home in death. Many who survived were dehumanised, treated as mere cargo. The crew held women and children above deck and abused them, while the crew members had the men perform dances for exercise and prevent a rebellion.

It is well-known what happened to those slaves who entered the New World and how the history of slavery still affects their descendants today. However, what is not always known is the Transatlantic slave trade effect on the future of Africa. The continent not only lost tens of millions of its skilled population, but the long-term demographic change was even more important since most of the slaves taken were men. The African states, whose markets they had come to control, collapsed when the slave trade was eventually abolished in the Americas and Europe, leaving them vulnerable to invasion and colonialism. The increased rivalry and influx of European arms had also fuelled the war and chaos that persists to this day. Apparently, Nigerians teach about their role in the slave trade:

"Many Nigerian middlemen began to depend totally on the slave trade and neglected every other business and occupation. The result was that when the trade was abolished [by England in 1807], these Nigerians began to protest. As years went by and the trade collapsed such Nigerians lost their sources of income and became impoverished."[40]

---

39 (Porter E. S., Speech For The 400-Years Seminar , 2019)

40 (Omolewa)

The Transatlantic slave trade has also led to the rise of colonial politics. Most African slavery had no more profound reason other than legal punishment or intertribal warfare. However, the Europeans who preached a universal philosophy, and who had long ago outlawed enslaving fellow Christians, needed justification for the practice so obviously at odds with their equality ideals. Consequently, they believed that Africans were biologically inferior and destined to be slaves by making numerous attempts to explain this theory. Slavery has since gained a racial base in Europe and the Americas, making it difficult for slaves and their potential heirs to gain equal status in society.

The Transatlantic slave trade was, on a massive scale, and injustice with a contingent consequence. Accordingly, Ghanaian diplomat Kofi Awoonor wrote:

"I believe there is a great psychic shadow over Africa, and it has much to do with our guilt and denial of our role in the slave trade. We too are blameworthy in what was essentially one of the most heinous crimes in human history."[41]

The question that is always lurking in the subconscious mind is: *how could Africans have sold other Africans into slavery?* The answer is that African slaveholders did not think of themselves or their slaves as 'Africans.' Instead they thought of themselves as Edo or Songhai, or other group members. They thought of their slaves as **foreigners or inferiors**. Similarly, the Spanish, the French, and the English could massacre each other in bloody wars because they thought of themselves as Spanish, French, or English, rather than Europeans. The difference is that the Europeans provided reparations or compensation to their losing European cousins after the war. In contrast, most African countries have not owned up claiming responsibility or accountability for their part in this horrific crime.

The above passage simply shows how the Children of Israel were enslaved by people who looked like them. "They thought of their slaves as foreigners or inferiors" simply suggests that the undefended communities of Israelites were *attacked* and raided and the inhabitants were treated as a commodity.

Another interesting bread crumb came during the early part of 1910 CE; a book called the "Negroes in the New World." It described the Elamites of Mesopotamia as having been a negroid people with kinky hair and transmitted this racial type to the Jews and Syrians. The description describes the curliness of the hair, and something called 'negro eye' and full lips in the portraiture of Assyria, which conveys an evident negro element in Babylonia. According to the reference on page 27:

---

41 (Johnson, 1994)

"1 The Jews are composed of three or four separate racial elements. The Asiatic negroid strain shows itself occasionally in the curly hair, the long eye, and proportions of the skull. The Jewish hybrids with the Negro in Jamaica and Guiana reproduce most strikingly the Assyrian type {supra}. 2 It is quite conceivable that the great peninsula of Arabia was once populated, as far as its natural conditions allowed, by a primitive negro stock, which may have been later on partially exterminated by changing and unfavourable conditions of climate and by the after-coming of the white man in his type."[42]

The above quote clearly shows the physical identity of the children of Israel living in the Americas, concluding that those brought from Africa were indeed the descendants of the children of Israel.

The Indian Connection

The world is still having difficulty grasping the simplest of concepts. Even with all of the proof, they refuse to believe what is presented, offering instead silly contradictions, which goes unchallenged. The Israelites were Black, not tanned or olive-skinned, not Yemeni Black, not light-skinned Black, just plain and simply Black. As if I said to you, *'it was THAT BLACK MAN'*, the image that your mind just conjured up with those words is the same that would apply to the Israelites of old - there is no shame, mystery or wisdom to this fact, it is what it is. I am though, often conflicted with this statement, because it should not and does not matter what colour the truth is; however, it is vital to acknowledge the foundation of this truth with the same breath. While India does not play a massive part in this discussion, it helps identify some of the challenges we are currently facing. Israelites were in India, actually a little state in the southern region of India bordering the Arabian Palencia, called Kerala.

There are aspects of the Hindu traditions, like many communities in the world, that contain Israelite traditions. India was one of the many countries that were influenced by King Solomon's kingdom-ship.

The Malabar Jews, from the city of Cochin in the southern Indian state of Kerala are said to be the oldest group of Jews in India. When one uses the term 'Malabari Jew' it is often synonymous with 'Black Jew'. Point to note: In the 15th and 16th century, when the self-proclaimed European Jews arrived in Kerala, not only did they look down upon the Israelites, who were present in Kerala when they arrived, they also referred to them as 'Black Jews' or 'Malabari Jews'. They did this to denote them, to say that they were *the*

---

42 (Johnston, 1910, p. 27)

other and they did not mix with them (such as India's caste system today). Benjamin of Tudela (1907), writes in his Itinerary, about the Kerala region of India:

"...throughout the island, including all the towns thereof, live several thousand Israelites. The inhabitants are all black, and the Jews also …… They know the law of Moses and the prophets."

These people later became known as the Malabari Jews. The Jacobites claim to have settled there from King Solomon's time. The Jacobites mixed with the natives of the land, yet some maintained their Israelite culture. However, the European Jews did not mix with the natives and definitely not with the Jacobites, as mentioned above.

According to the scriptures, especially during King Solomon's time (reigned around 970 to 931 BCE), often spoke of goods coming from Ophir, such as spices, perfumes, plants, animals, textiles, trees like the algum tree and precious stones, such as onyx and sapphire and gold. Ophir may have been the Coptic name for India, which is Sophir. According to the books, **1 Kings** and **2 Chronicles,** ships often came from Ophir bringing merchandise[43]. Also, the algum tree itself may have been sandalwood, which is native to southern India. The distance from old Jerusalem to India is therefore justified by the location.

Around four hundred years later, following the destruction of the First Temple during the Siege of Jerusalem (587 BC), some Israelite exiles may have travelled and settled in India. During the time of King Ahasuerus (Xerxes I of Persia 519–465 BCE), India was mentioned as one of his provinces,

"Now it came to pass in the days of Ahasuerus, (this is Ahasuerus which reigned, from India even unto Ethiopia, over an hundred and seven and twenty provinces:)" -Esther **1:1.**

However, messengers sent the letter in which Mordecai had written in the kings' name (as persuaded by queen Esther) to every province instructing the Israelites to protect themselves. Later on, they received letters to celebrate this momentous occasion, calling it Purim. By this time, travelling was a little more practical and central Persia (modern-day Iran), was a lot closer to India. Nevertheless, according to local South Indian legends, the Jacobites in this region came during the first-century CE., after King Solomon's second temple's destruction.

---

[43] Thundy, Zacharias P. " India and the West in Antiquity". *Buddha and Christ.* Leiden, The Netherlands: Brill, 1993.

Another well-known influx of settlers came around the time of the Portuguese during the Spanish and Portuguese inquisition: These were known as the Sephardic Jews and others who emigrated from the Middle East, Persia, Yemen, and Europe. Then came the European Jews, including Germans, known as the *Paradesis*, a word that means 'foreigners' in Malayalam (a native language spoken in this region of India). The Paradesis leveraged the caste system to maintain their separate identity and became known as "White Jews."

The Jacobites in Cochin were persecuted under Portuguese rule (1498-1663). However, under Dutch rule (1663-1795), they gained better status, and since the British settled mainly in Mumbai and Calcutta, Kerala's economy plummeted, so many of the locals moved to other cities. And of course, the good ole missionaries came and did their thing, totally corrupting the people with their strange Christian philosophy.

Kerala is known to be one of India's most literate states, where the people are laid back friendly and welcoming. Many families that claim Israelite heritage left Kerala/India during the transplantation into the Israeli colony. Still, most Jacobites were assimilated into the other dominant cultures, and today there are very few Israelite families living there. Prior to the assimilation, many Indian people became indentured labourers and were taken to many countries across the world, especially after the abolishment of slavery. Like the Cape Coast in Ghana, Cochin was one of the major trading ports of Kerala. Therefore, I would not be surprised if a few descendants from the Jacobites ended up becoming indentured labourers and joining their long-lost cousins in places like Guyana, Trinidad and Jamaica, who were brought as slaves from West Africa.

Conclusion

Now, certain prophecies had to be fulfilled, for instance:

1. **Genesis 15:13** talks about the 400 years enslavement. It is important to note that although Israel spent 430 years in Egypt, only about half of that time were they enslaved; they also ruled Egypt, forming the 15th to the 16th Dynasties. This means that the 400 hundred years of affliction had not occurred during the old Egypt. Porter always emphasised that there were no other nations taken into captivity throughout history and served their captures for 400 years. [44]
2. **Leviticus 26:14-45** talks about the punishment for our disobedience (slavery).
3. **Deuteronomy 28:15-68:** talks about our punishment, enslavement, and the voyage to the new Egypt. These scriptures are fascinating as we have seen in the previous

---

[44] (Porter, The Truth, The Lie and The Bible, 1995)

parts how the brutality of the children of Israel mirrored that of verses 15 to 67. Finally, Verse 68 is so profound that it undeniably identifies the progenitors of this prophecy.

Therefore, it is clear that the Israelites that left Israel prior, during and shortly after 70 CE are the same Israelites that travelled around Europe, the Mediterranean, Asia, and taken to West Africa. They set up industries and taught their skills and craft and helped to build cities and great civilisations. These same Israelites were also envied and persecuted heavily, forced to serve foreign gods, **"….never finding ease among the nations."** So, they became **"… an astonishment, a proverb, and a byword, among all nations…"** found in **Deuteronomy 28:67 & 37.**

Chapter Four

Post Slavery

After the Civil War in the United States, the nation tended to adopt many hitherto southern attitudes on the racial question. It is perhaps one of the most extraordinary anomalies of our history that the North, the undisputed victor of the war, treated the South, not as a traitor, not punishing them as a traitor, but as a source of imitation.

In his analysis of the post-war reconstruction era, which he calls an "ultraconservative revolution," Eric McKittrick, points out that the United States spent most of its energy, in the early years of peace, on amnesty, pardoning southerners. He says that much less has been done for emancipated slaves through land distribution and social planning than for liberated serfs in imperial Russia. He recounts how the North seemed more intent on appeasing the South than on treating the newly liberated Jacobites fairly:

"Once the war was over, the problem of dealing both with the Negro and with the readmission of Southern states to the Federal Union dominated all else. But all emphasis was placed on the latter. And again, the first instinct was to change as little as possible. By constitutional amendment, the Negro had been given his freedom, but few steps were taken to adjust him to his new status. At the same time, elaborate efforts were made by the administration of Lincoln's successor, Andrew Johnson, to re-establish state governments in the South which would be more or less identical with those in existence before the war. Certain things were rejected almost out of hand. There was no redistribution of land, either with or without compensation. There was no insistence that Negroes be accorded rights of citizenship. Federal responsibility for education and welfare was regarded as being only of the most temporary and limited kind."[45]

During the late 1860s and early 1870s, a program called 'Radical Reconstruction' was adopted. The government designed these measures to protect the Jacobites and those whites in the South who had supported the Union. Federal troops occupied the South, and martial law was in force. The entire Jacobite male population was given the right to vote, former Confederate leaders were temporarily banned from voting or holding office,

---

45 1.Eric McKittrick, "Reconstruction: Ultraconservative Revolution," in C. Vann Woodward (ed.), The Comparative Approach to American History, (N.Y.: Basic Books, Inc., 1SW), p.151.

and state governments were formed that were heavily dependent on the Jacobite's votes. This system was suddenly undermined when President Rutherford B. Hayes ordered the Federal troops withdrawn in 1877.

Whites in the South, forced to accept measures they did not want, moved quickly to reinstate the old regime. They could do so relatively soon because the temporary programmes had not been supported by anything systematic, regarding social and economic prosperity. There have been no widespread efforts to help those released acquire their shares. Priorities had been reversed. The Jacobites had been given the vote before they had education or the economic power to use it. Even if one argues that political rights should have come first after the federal government was unwilling to commit itself to preserve those rights.

By the late 1870s, the political, social, and economic systems of the South had come to resemble their counterparts of the pre-war era. But, now the Jacobites were a landless labourer, rather than a legally-bound slave. In gaining his "freedom" he had lost his place in the social system. In slavery, he had a measure of security and protection; following Reconstruction, he had none. His small political gains and minimal social rights were systematically removed.

"One by one, and with no interference whatever, the Southern states now began by law to impose systems of social segregation and disfranchisement which set the Negro entirely outside the mainstream of Southern civic life. By 1900, the process was virtually complete."[46]

We find that every conceivable hurdle was thrown in the way of the newly released children of slavery in the last quarter of the 19th century. In many ways, their situation was worse during this period than it had been under slavery. They were now being ostracised and segregated. The laws designed to protect them were genuinely ignored, and the Jim Crow laws became more numerous and more vigorously enforced with each passing year. It was indeed the base; it was a time when any of the children of slavery was fair game for abuse at any white person's hands.

It is not surprising then that the Jacobites turned to their inner Spiritual self at this time. Their spirituality had always played a prominent role in their lives and their descendants.

---

46 The slaves' rebellion

It has doubtless been a source of strength and comfort to them during the tormented history in the Americas. Furthermore, they have in them a deep inclination towards spirituality and servitude. The slaves were Christianised soon after they arrived in America. They adopted Christianity with a cruel passion and have been the most consistently devout Christians that the world has ever seen.

In retrospect, however, it seems strange that the Jacobites and their descendants adopted Christianity with such conviction; after all, it is the slave masters' philosophy. There was, and still is, something disturbing about learning the Christian message of universal love from a people that held your people in cruel bondage. Nevertheless, it was not the privilege of the slaves to choose their philosophy of choice; slave masters encouraged or forced their slaves to convert. Many slave masters saw the advantage of a pious slave as many valued their master's life over their own.

It should be noted that even though the vast population of Jacobites attended the Christian churches, many did so as a form of social gathering. It was a reason to get dressed up, go out, and spend time with friends and family – in other words, going to church for some had nothing to do with the Christian
philosophy; it was about socializing. While many slaves accepted this form of religious instruction, many gave their Masters the impression that they did. However, there were significant Jacobite responses to the Christian philosophy during the 19th century, which went beyond submissiveness to outright defiance of one sort or another.

Most slaves accepted this form of religious instruction or gave their Masters the impression that they did. However, there were significant Jacobite responses to the Christian philosophy during the 19th century, which went beyond submissiveness to outright defiance of one sort or another.

Chapter Five

Insurrections

Gabriel Prosser: Slave Rebellion - August 30, 1800

In Richmond, Virginia, Gabriel, a 24-year-old blacksmith slave of Thomas Prosser, commenced with organising a slave revolt during what is now known as Freedom Month (August). He planned to kill the whites of the area, seize arms and ammunition from the arsenal in Richmond and strike an agreement with the slave masters for the liberation of all slaves.[47]

The one thousand slaves who were gathered to revolt disbanded in confusion when a tremendous storm struck that night. Like many biblical leaders, Gabriel's plot was doomed to fail because two slaves had revealed the plan to their masters for the state's reward. The slaves did not receive full compensation. Gabriel, his two brothers (Solomon and Martin), and 23 other slaves, were hanged.

Gabriel was a student of the Bible and based his desire to lead an insurrection on his religious convictions. His favourite Biblical hero was Samson, and in imitation of the great Israelite leader, he wore his hair long. He believed that from his childhood, God had marked him as a deliverer of his people. He is said to have connected the enslaved Jacobites in America with the Bible and taught the earliest iteration of Jacobites being God's people.[48] [49]

Denmark Vesey: Slave Rebellion - July 14, 1822

Denmark Vesey was a slave who had won one thousand five hundred dollars in a lottery and bought his freedom from his master for six hundred dollars, the same year of the Gabriel insurrection. He had sailed with his master to the Virgin Islands and Haiti for

---

[47] https://muse.jhu.edu/article/488336/summary

[48] https://www.pbs.org/wgbh/aia/part3/3p1576.html

[49] Douglas R. Egerton (1993). Gabriel's Rebellion: The Virginia Conspiracies of 1800 and 1802. Chapel Hill, NC: University of North Carolina Press. pp. 21–22.
https://archive.org/details/gabrielsrebellio0000eger/page/21

twenty years. His travels brought him into contact with the Jacobites of South Carolina. In 1822, Vesey organised several thousand Jacobites, equipped only with homemade weapons, in an attack on Charleston's whites and its vicinity.

Like Gabriel's, the conspiracy was uncovered by an overzealous slave, which gave the militia plenty of time to move around the city and surround it. Within thirty days, one hundred and thirty-one persons had been arrested, thirty-seven executed, including Vesey himself, forty-three banished from the state or the country, and forty-eight whipped and discharged. All this without any white person having been struck a blow.

Like Gabriel, Vesey was a student of the Bible, and he brought to his reading some highly unorthodox interpretations, perhaps of African or West Indian origin, for white people. He predominantly studied two passages from the Old Testament, one being the account of Joshua's siege of the Canaanite city of Jericho. With his intuition and knowledge of the Scriptures, Vesey saw many parallels between the children of Israel and slavery.

Like all the Israelites' battles, Joshua's was a holy war, and Vesey was convinced the same was true for the slaves he had been called to lead to freedom. Vesey was fascinated by the biblical stories and often used them in his speeches to the Jacobites in Charleston. At these religious meetings, he used Biblical accounts to give his listeners self-respect and courage.

Nat Turner: Slave Rebellion - August 21, 1831

Nat Turner was born into slavery on October 2, 1800, eight days before Gabriel Prosser was executed. Known as the *Prophet*, he raised one of the most successful slave rebellions during his time. He claimed that God instructed him to rebel. In his confession, he states,

"On May 12, 1828, I heard a loud noise in the heavens and the spirit instantly appeared to me and said the serpent was loosened, and Christ had laid down the yoke he had born for the sins of man and that I should take it on and fight against the serpent for the time was fast approaching when the first should be last, and the last should be first, and by signs in the heavens that it would make known to me when I should commence the great work and until the first sign appeared I should concede it from the knowledge of men and on the appearance of the sign the eclipse of the Sun last February 1831 I should arise and prepare myself and slay my enemies with their own weapons and immediately on the sign appearing in the heavens the seal was removed from my lips, and I communicated the great work laid out for me to do to 4 in whom I had the greatest confidence."[50]

Note that the sign came during the new moon, as we recognise a solar eclipse that can only occur during an astronomical new moon. With a group of six men, he killed his master and everyone in the house. They seized his guns and ammunition, and a few days later, at least seventy slaves were involved in the killing of around sixty whites in Southampton County. Turner and his group became fugitives, and by the end of October, he was captured.

According to his confession, Turner was betrayed by two slaves who had stumbled on his hiding place. After being sentenced, he was asked if he regretted what he had done, and he responded, "Was Christ not crucified?" He was eventually hanged on November 11, 1831, in *Jerusalem*, Virginia, then decapitated and skinned. His skin was probably given to onlookers as a souvenir[51].

The revolt led to a wave of fear and panic throughout the South and increased the desire for liberty on the part of the slaves. The effect on the free exercise of Jacobite's religion was immediate. Laws were passed prohibiting the slaves from learning to read and write and forbidding them to preach, upon pain of whipping. This constraint prompted free Jacobites to leave white churches and to begin to assemble their own.

It was not only the Jacobites insurrectionaries of the nineteenth century who were influenced by the Bible and the Second Testament. Many Jacobite leaders of that time made repeated references to the Israelites, usually by way of explicit comparison with the Jacobite people of America; some made an implicit reference to Judaism by rejecting the type of Christianity practised in America. Nevertheless, many still considered themselves Christians and few, except those mentioned earlier, recognised themselves as descendants or related to the ancient Israelites.

---

50 Slave Insurrection in Southampton County, Va., Headed by Nat Turner, With an Interesting Letter from a Fugitive Slave to His Old Master Jan 1850 Wesleyan Book Room P10

https://books.google.com.sa/books?id=f2VHAQAAMAAJ&pg=PP23&dq=nat+turner&hl=en&sa=X&ved=2ahUKEwi7qNf2_KDtAhU0TxUIHeinD5QQ6AEwAXoECAcQAg#v=onepage&q&f=true

51 https://www.nytimes.com/2016/10/18/opinion/nat-turners-skull-and-my-students-purse-of-skin.html

Chapter Six

Cultural Identity

After the numerous insurrections that occurred during slavery, it appeared that many of the Jacobite community leaders settled for the Christian philosophy; embracing a white Jesus as their God. However, at the beginning of the 20th century onwards, the Jacobites began to perceive Christianity as an instrument of white oppression. The idealistic Christian doctrine of salvation seemed impossible to attain for the Jacobites and always contradicted his actual life.

As a result, the Jacobites started to link his history to the biblical Israelites, just like Gabriel Prosser, Denmark Vesey and Nat Turner. The Jacobites went from a quest of identification, to the biblical children of Israel, to a symbolic relationship, and then to the actual claims of physical descent. This era also continued to nurture the church as a place for cultural expression as it served the diverse needs of the Jacobite communities. It was a beacon of hope to some and a suitable location for socializing, providing education and sharing resources for others. It was also a gathering spot for discussion on equality, freedom, racial and social justice.

Many church leaders encompassed a duality role, because when it seemed as though they were preaching the Christian philosophy, they raised the awareness of the injustices, while preaching the comparison between the Israelites of old and the Jacobite's current situation. Hence, the birth of the civil rights movement, where leaders, such as Dr. Martin Luther King Jr. and Malcolm X, made their entrance onto the world stage, forever changing the Jacobites' narrative. Even though Malcolm X was a spokesperson for
the Nation of Islam, and not a Christian, his father was an outspoken Baptist preacher and devoted supporter of Marcus Garvey. It is clear to see the buildup of frustrated Jacobite leaders desperately trying to establish an identity while making sense of their current situation. The eventual establishment of the BHI movement, or Black Jewish communities, operating on the rhetoric of awareness or the Exodus, took form in the 1960s and early 70s.

The BHI combined the philosophies and world views of Black nationalism and Judaism and the return to Africa movement inspired by Marcus Garvey and Ben Amin Ben Israel. They started their teachings of the Jacobite diaspora and biblical history between the late 1920s to the late 1960s when Ben Israel finally took a few hundred individuals back to Africa.

According to the Ben Israel doctrine, the Jacobites in the diaspora came from Israel, which was originally Eden in the continent of Africa. They migrated during the Roman conquest to West Africa. Many of them were eventually enslaved and shipped to the Americas and the Caribbean. While their roots in Israel and Africa were cut by the slave trade, they never recovered and can only recover by returning to Jerusalem and the African motherland.

Many of these BHI organisations are fashioned after Judaism; this, however, is a grave error. Some may even have elements of Christianity or Islam, both of which should also be of major concern. First of all, as mentioned above, Christianity is indeed the instrument of oppression and damnation for the Jacobites. Everything about Christianity is contrary to the development, identity and spirituality of the Jacobites. The masonic Christian philosophy and its detrimental effects on the Jacobites are discussed at length in Elder Shadrock Porter's books.

Secondly, Islamic philosophy borrows many of the Israelite customs and traditions. This is not surprising, as some would argue, it was Khadijah, the wealthy Israelite[52] merchant and wife to Mohammed, who first taught him the Israelite customs, along with her cousin, Waraqah[53]; however, that is a story for another day.

Finally, in the Chapter 'Speaking Hebrew', we identified a few crucial points that have a significant bearing on the proceeding BHI movements:

1.   Christianity created Judaism. Why then would you want to adopt the practices of a philosophy developed by the system, which in its nature is not only contrary to one's existence, but is also oppressive?

---

52 (Wikipedia, 2005) (Wikipedia, Khadija bint Khuwaylid, 2005)

53 Waraqah may have helped Muhammad develop the religion that he would preach; Waraqah, died a few days after meeting meeting Muhammed and discussing his vision .

2.	The language that represents Judaism is a modern-day vernacular that was recently created.

3.	The real reason Christianity created Judaism has to do with the great whores' master plan for deceiving the nations, especially the true people of God, the Israelites. For, if the Jews are white, as the entire world currently perceives them to be, then who would believe the Jacobite when he tries to claim back his identity. Especially when he follows the Ashkenazi Jewish language and dress. Unfortunately, most of the Jacobite is still in denial of his true identity.

4.	Furthermore, even though some of these BHI groups denounce Judaism, they hold steadfast to its Israeli Hebrew Language and its God, Yahweh. As we discovered, in the section 'Israeli Hebrew Language', the true name for Satan is Yahweh.

5.	BHI tend to follow the custom of changing one's name without understanding that this is a great error.

In the KJV Bible, there are many examples of great men that glorified God without the need to change their names. For instance, Moses is an Egyptian name. Joseph and Daniel also had non-Israelite names that were given to them. Hadassah's Babylonian name was Esther and one of the books of the Bible is named after her. Ruth never changed her name to become a full-fledged Israelite. Names are usually given by those who have authority over you; for instance, your parents, the slave master and God. It was the God of Israel that changed Abram's name to Abraham, named Isaac and surnamed Jacob, Israel. Even Saul's Israelite name was changed to the gentile name Paul. He did not change it. Yet, the inventor of the Israeli Hebrew Language changed his own name when assuming the Israeli identity and BHI members seem to follow suit. Also, the Catholic's use this practice because they understand the spiritual connotation, changing someone's name is to have power over them.

A final point is the return to Africa or Israel movement that many of these BHI organisations promote. This is an erroneous narrative of biblical, historical and prophetic proportions. Africa is not the Jacobites home, neither was it promised to him. It was prophesied that the Jacobites would see the land Israel, his homeland, *no more again*. The land is now occupied, owned and operated by Israelis, and to that point, it was prophesied that Israel would see that land no more again, this is emphasized in the book of kings.

"Then will I cut off Israel out of the land which I have given them; and this house, which I have hallowed for my name, will I cast out of my sight; and Israel shall be a proverb and a byword among all people" -1 Kings 9:7

Therefore, to say that most of these organisations are wrong in their narrative or rhetoric is an understatement. They have merely jumped out of the frying pan into the fire, moving from Christianity to Judaism with its made-up Israeli Hebrew language.

This section explores the historical development of several groups that embrace Judaism or adopt the Hebrew noun as part of their identity. The list of Black Hebrew communities offered here is not complete. Rather, it identifies some of the major communities and presents various approaches towards their practices, culture and identity. Also, discussion of their media attention, their relationship with mainstream Judaism, Christianity or even Islam are outlined as well.

Chapter Seven

Black Nationalist and BHI Movements

Many BHI adhere to a strict hierarchical structure, with clearly defined roles and responsibilities and gender segregation. The roles and classifications may include: bishop, deacon, high priest, chief priest, apostle, captain, officer, soldier and brother. Bishops and other high-ranking members are regarded as divine and trustworthy sources of truth. Women in the group can organise their activities and are referred to as *sisters*. In many BHI camps, women are not allowed to wear trousers or fraternise with male members. Marriage between members of the group is encouraged and celebrated.

Most BHI organisations serve the deity Yahweh and follow Judaism, with hints of Islam and Christianity. They all learn to speak or use words from the modern-day Israeli Hebrew language. Simultaneously, they claim to identify with the Children of Israel in the KJV Bible. They all refer to themselves as Hebrew Israelites or BHI.

Church of God and Saints of Christ (COGSOC)

Founder: William Saunders Crowdy
Date: 1896
Website: https://www.cogasoc.org/
Location: Lawrence, Kansas
God: Yahweh
Philosophy: Christian organisations, based on Judaism, utilise the first and second testaments.

One of the oldest BHI organisations in the Americas that adheres to the tenets of Judaism was founded by William Saunders Crowdy, an American soldier, preacher, entrepreneur, and pastor. Crowdy was born into slavery on August 11, 1847, in St. Mary County, Maryland. Basil Crowdy, his father, was a profoundly devout Christian who oversaw clay drying on the plantation. It was illegal for slaves to read; however, he learned to read the Bible at an early age. At the age of 16 or 17, Crowdy fled from the plantation and joined the Union army to fight for the freedom of slaves. He shed the Wilson name, regarding it as a name for a slave, and became Crowdy.[54]

---

[54] (Gallagher & Ashcraft, 2006) p62

In 1867, Crowdy was a soldier in the military with the fifth cavalry. He eventually settled down in Guthrie, Oklahoma, following a career as a cook on the Santa Fe Railroad. He married and raised a family. On September 13, 1892, Crowdy had his first vision. God came to him in the field and told him to lead his people, the Jacobites, to the True Religion. By that time, the slave world was over; however, the world of slavery, under prejudice, bigotry, and hatred, was never far from the children of slavery's experience. In 1895, three years later, Crowdy was chopping wood when he had another vision that terrified him greatly.[55]

God, according to Crowdy, proceeded to reveal his *Ancient Plan of Salvation* in a vision. Apparently, in his visions, he discovered the Lost Tribes of Israel were the Black Man of Africa, especially the former slaves of the United States. The Americas' former slaves were the true inheritor of Israel and the Promised Land, not the modern Ashkenazi Jews. Crowdy taught the Jacobites to keep the Ten Commandments: Love one another, pay their honest debts, and abstain from alcohol and tobacco. Although he thought the children of slavery were God's people, he mixed aspects of Christianity and tenants of Judaism with the slave narratives. Known as one of the earliest BHI in the United States, Crowdy's established the Church of God and Saints of Christ in 1896, after he claimed to have had visions telling him "that Blacks were descendants of the twelve lost tribes of Israel."[56] [57]

A fundamental difference for Crowdy was his message of Black nationalism, Black affirmation and positive identity that was independent of the *white man's world*. Crowdy's message was no longer dependent on the white man's god or identity to legitimise himself. He defined a concept, later co-opted by other Jacobites, which is *Black is beautiful*.[58]

Crowdy moved his family from Guthrie to Lawrence, Kansas in 1896, and founded his first church in Lawrence. The Lawrence Church brought in many receptive converts to Crowdy's message. His word continued to spread. Within three years of his arrival in

---

[55] https://www.cogasoc.org/leaders/prophet-william-s-crowdy/ (COGASOC, 2020)

[56] (Eugene V. Gallagher, 2011) p. 62.

[57] (Bleich, 1975) Crowdy claimed to be the recipient of a series of revelations in which, among other things, he was told that Blacks were descendants of the ten lost tribes of Israel.

[58] (Klinger, 2020) retrieved Nov 15, 2020 p3

Kansas, Crowdy's Church of God and Saints of Christ was organised in 29 different Kansas towns. The congregation later established locations in Africa, Cuba and the Caribbean. The male members wear yarmulkes (Khazarian headdress), and all members adhere to Judaism as their religion, even though the organisation is closely affiliated with Christianity.[59] The members are referred to as Black Jews; however, they are slowly changing their narrative, claiming the God of Abraham, Isaac and Jacob instead of Yahweh.

But, as per their website dated Jan 1, 2021, Yahweh is still their god, "We believe in the existence of God the Creator, the Eternal, the Absolute Ruler of the Universe, the God Yahweh revealed to our father Abraham, who is One alone and who alone is to be worshipped and glorified. To God, the Creator only do we pray."[60]

The Temple of the Gospel of the Kingdom
Founder: Warren Roberson
Date: 1900
Location: Virginia, Harlem
God: Yahweh
Philosophy: Black Nationalist organisation based on Judaism.

The Temple of the Gospel of the Kingdom was founded in 1900, in Virginia, by Warren Roberson. They followed an Ashkenazi Jewish orthodoxy culture and studied Yiddish. The Temple established their "kingdom" in Harlem and another branch in Atlantic City in 1917. Communal living and celibacy were part of their belief system which claimed members would enjoy eternal life on earth.[61] The organisation collapsed shortly after that because Robertson was charged and imprisoned for legal and moral issues. He was involved in the transportation of women across state lines for immoral purposes and sentenced to eighteen months in prison. Additionally, women had allegedly borne children for the leader, giving rise to controversy, as the media reported it to be a *baby farm*[62].

---

[59] (Klinger, 2020) retrieved Nov 15, 2020

[60] https://www.cogasoc.org/about/this-we-believe-2/ (This We Believe, 2020). Reference to their God *Yahweh* retrieved December 4, 2020

[61] (Toby Widdicombe, 2017) p. 391

[62] (Konighofer, 2008) p.109

Church of the Living God

Founder: Frank S. Cherry
Date: 1917
Website: https://cotlghqindy.org
Location: Philadelphia
God: Yahweh
Philosophy: Judaism, Christianity, including the Trinity, and the Talmud.

The Church of the Living God, the Pillar and Ground for Truth of All Nations was founded by Frank S. Cherry[63],[64] a former seaman and railroad worker. Cherry read and wrote Yiddish. He too transferred his ministry around 1917 to Philadelphia, where he was inspired by the Church of God and the Saints of Christ. He formed his own more anti-White theological direction by teaching that God, Jesus, the Ancient Israelites were Jacobites.[65]

They believe that white people are descended from Ghazi, a light-skinned Black man who was cursed. Members believed that the European Jews were impostors, and his followers were the true Israelites. Yet, they practised Judaism by observing the Saturday Sabbath, the Passover, prohibited pork in their diets, forbade divorce and photography and embraced the cross. Members argued that Judaism is a tradition associated with Africa, and the descendants of slaves are connected to the original Children of Israel. Tenets of his church included Black Nationalism and support for Marcus Garvey.[66]

Commandment Keepers

Founder: Wentworth A. Matthew
Date: 1919
Website: https://www.commandmentkeepersehc.org/
Location: Harlem, New York City
God: YHWH
Philosophy: Judaism - strict Orthodox Hebrew teaching and keeping with the laws of the Torah.
Identity: Ethiopian Hebrews. Men and boys will wear a kippah, skullcap, or yarmulke.

---

[63] (Pinn, African American Religious Culture: Volume 1 A-R, 2009)

[64] Ibid p. 167

[65] (Klinger, 2020) p4

[66] Ibid p167—168

Wentworth Arthur Matthew established the Commandment Keepers in Harlem, New York. He primarily based his learning on Judaism and rejected all New Testament teachings, even though he took the title of Rabbi and ordained Rabbis in his congregation. Matthew and the Commandment Keepers pursued acceptance from the Ashkenazi Jewish establishments, including the New York Board of Rabbis; however, while his efforts were unsuccessful, Matthew himself reported feeling outcast by the Ashkenazi Jews. Matthew supported accepting Jewish refugees and encouraged harmony between his group and the Ashkenazi Jews. The congregation started in 1919, in Harlem, New York, before becoming a synagogue.[67]

Wentworth Arthur Matthews was born in the Caribbean in 1892. He claimed to have been born in Lagos, Nigeria, however, others believe he was born in the Caribbean, in St. Kitts[68]. He founded the Commandment Keepers in 1919, in Harlem. It has been said that "Matthew modelled his congregation on the white Judaism he saw around him in New York."[69] Learning about the Beta Israel community, the Ethiopian Jewish community, he added another personalised Black international link to his developing Jewish philosophy.

Central to Rabbi Matthew's views on Jews was that the children of slavery were the original Jews. European Jews were the descendants of the fabled Jewish conversion kingdom of the Khazars in Central Asia. However, members of the Commandments Keepers closely adhered to traditional Ashkenazi Judaism, practised Kashrut, observed the Sabbath, circumcised their male children, and abstained from pork. Like in the orthodox Ashkenazi Jewish tradition, men and women were seated separately, and orthodox Ashkenazi Jewish prayer books in Hebrew/Yiddish are used.[70]

The Torah and the Talmud are central to the Commandment Keeper's daily life. The Commandment Keeper's conversions of the children of slavery to Judaism were not considered conversions by them. They were considered much more simply as a *return to their roots*. Christianity was rejected, placing the Commandment Keepers well outside of the mainstream of American Black religious life. Matthew established the Ethiopian Hebrew Rabbinical College (later renamed the Israelite Rabbinical Academy) in Brooklyn.

---

67 (Klinger, 2020) p6

68 (Chafets, 2009)

69 (Chafets, 2009)

70 (Levy, 2017)

Besides the Harlem group, there are about ten Commandment Keeper congregations in the New York area, and others exist throughout North America and Israel. No matter how much the Commandment Keepers adhered to traditional Judaism, they and Rabbi Matthew were never accepted by mainstream Judaism as part of the historical traditional Jewish world. Matthew eventually concluded Black Jews would never be accepted as equals by the Ashkenazi Jewish community. The rejection of Matthew, and other self-adopted Black Jewish communities, as Jews by the Ashkenazi Jewish world, has led to a further distancing.[71]

After Rabbi Matthew's death in 1973, Rabbi Capers Funnye took over the mantle of rabbinical leadership of the shrinking community of Commandment Keepers. Rabbi Funnye founded and took over the pulpit of the Ethiopian-Hebrew Beth Shalom B'nai Zaken congregation in Chicago. Ironically, he is a cousin of Michele Obama, President Obama's wife.

Rabbi Funnye is accepted as a Rabbi by the Chicago Board of Rabbis today. Some say this was done for various reasons, including liberal Jewish values, or political expediency. However, the distance between Rabbi Funnye's BHI Jewish community and the Ashkenazi Jewish community has not narrowed.

Universal Negro Improvement Association and African Communities League (UNIA)

Founder: Marcus Garvey
Date: 1919
Website: https://www.unia-acl.org
Location: Philadelphia
Philosophy: Christianity, Back to Africa Movement, Black Nationalist.

Marcus Garvey, a highly controversial Jamaican Black Nationalist, headed the Universal Negro Improvement Association and African Communities League in New York, known as UNIA. Until 1919, Garvey was an essential influence on the children of slavery's life in America as editor of the *Negro World* newspaper, with a circulation of 2,000,000 copies. Garvey called for a movement to return to Africa. Duse Mohammed Ali, a British actor, journalist and fervent Muslim missionary in London, had a profound influence on him,. Garvey allied himself with white supremacists, the KKK and the notorious racist Senator Bilbo to bring the children of slavery back to Africa.

---

71 (Pinn, African American Religious Culture: Volume 1 A-R, 2009) p169

When Garvey was convicted of mail fraud, he blamed the Jews. Garvey told a journalist in 1928, "When they wanted to get me, they had a Jewish judge try me, and a Jewish prosecutor. I would have been freed, but two Jews on the jury held out against me ten hours and succeeded in convicting me, whereupon the Jewish judge gave me the maximum penalty." [72]

President Coolidge pardoned Garvey and he was deported to Jamaica. On November 15, 1964, the Government of Jamaica proclaimed Garvey its first national hero. He was reinterred in a shrine in National Heroes Park. The red, Black and green flag of the UNIA and African Communities League was adopted as the Black Liberation Flag commonly recognised in Jacobite communities.[73]

Rastafarians regard Garvey as a prophet. Rastafarians are a spiritual movement which emerged in Jamaica in the 1930s. They believe Haile Selassie I, Emperor of Ethiopia, is Jesus incarnate and the Second Advent of Jesus's reincarnation. Selassie ascended to the Ethiopian throne in 1930 and reigned until his death in 1974. Selassie was a Christian and adhered to the tenets and ritual of the Ethiopian Orthodox church. The Ethiopian Orthodox Church claims to possess the Ark of the Covenant. To believe that the God of Israel would give those He considered His enemies the holy vestige of the Israelites, the Ark of the Covenant, is a mistake. Even among the Israelites, one had to be sanctified and chosen even to touch the Ark of the Covenant, how much more, a people of a different culture, practice and background.

Throughout the 1920s Garvey spoke of a Black king that will be crowned who will mark the days of coming Black liberation. The only African king with thousands of years of documented history, who could his lineage back to King Solomon of Israel and the Queen of Sheba, was the Christian Emperor of the kingdom of Ethiopia, Haile Selassie I.[74]

In the 1970s and 1980s, in a daringly high-risk effort, the Israeli government brought home the surviving remnants of Ethiopian Jewry to Israel. They were threatened with destruction and extinction. The Israeli Law of Return applied to the Beta Israel, (Ethiopian

---

[72] (JUNE 23, 1923: MARCUS GARVEY'S TRIAL ENDS; HE HAS BEEN SENTENCED TO A FIVE-YEAR IMPRISONMENT, 2019)

[73] (Marcus Garvey (1887 - 1940), 2020)

[74] (Martin, 2009)

Jews -Community of Israel) after Halakhic (religious) and constitutional discussions affirmed their Jewish identity.

Over the centuries, the Ethiopian Jewish community has intermarried with the local peoples. They were racially Black, but they remained steadfastly loyal to their adopted Israelite cultural traits, beliefs and links to their identity for two thousand years. They are citizens of Israel today. They continue to struggle with the cultural challenges of Israeli life in the Western world.

The Moorish Zionist Temple of the Moorish Jew

Founder: Leon Richie Lou, then Israel Ben Newman and Mordecai Herman
Date: 1899, then 1923
Location: Harlem, NY with affiliate branches in Newark, New Jersey and Philadelphia, Pennsylvania
God: Yahweh
Philosophy: Orthodox Judaism.

Leon Richie Lou had originally founded the Moorish Zionist temple in 1899. It established a temple in Brooklyn, New York, which was recognised and reformed in 1921 under Mordecai Herman and Israel Ben Newman's leadership. Herman and Newman were followers of Marcus Garvey, and they established The Moorish Zionist temple of the Moorish Jews. They also followed Judaism teachings.

Herman was an actual member of Marcus Garvey's UNIA and was one of the first Jacobites to endorse a homeland for Black Jews in Palestine. Rabbi Arnold Josiah Ford later joined Rabbi Samuel Valentine and Rabbi Mordecai Herman. Rabbi Ford and Rabbi Samuel Valentine split in 1924. Rabbi Ford started the Beth B'nai Abraham and included Islam elements in his practice, writing prayers to Allah and observing Ramadan. His movement was Moorish-Israelite-Islamic-Free Masonic in nature.[75]

Dubious concepts surround the further developments of Ford. Some believe he died after a brief illness on the eve of the outbreak of the Italo-Ethiopian war, while others claim Ford returned to the United States under the name of Wallace D. Fard. Under the alias of Fard, Ford is said to have then established the nation of Islam, whose mythical founding story has also been related to the Moorish Science Temple of Noble Drew Ali.[76]

---

[75] (Mujaddid, 2020)

[76] (Sundquist, 2009) p116

Beth B'nai Abraham

Founder: Rabbi Arnold Josiah Ford
Date: 1927
Location: Ethiopia
God: Yahweh
Philosophy: Judaism with hints of Islam.

Arnold Josiah Ford and a small group of BHI went to Ethiopia, where they participated in Emperor Haile Selassie's coronation, created a school, and acquired 800 acres (320 ha) of land to unite BHI of the Diaspora with Ethiopians. Like many BHI leaders, Rabbi Arnold Josiah Ford immigrated from the Caribbean to the United States. He became an active member of Garvey's UNIA. Ford, a musician by training, was employed for a time in the British Navy, wrote the universal 'Ethiopian anthem of UNIA' and published the universal Ethiopian hymnal. Clashes with Garvey over royalties and politics led to their separation. He was a member of the Scottish Rite Masons where he served as Master of the Memmon Lodge. He married Olive Nurse, and the couple had two children before divorcing in 1924.[77]

Ford's life, and the interrelationships of different BHI in Harlem, is confusing and inconsistent. Some sources indicate Ford was an early convert to Rabbi Matthew's Commandment Keepers but had a falling out. Other sources claim Ford, who assumed the title of Rabbi from a vague origin, ordained Rabbi Matthew, so he could continue his work while in Ethiopia. Ford converted to Judaism in 1924.

He founded his synagogue in Harlem, the Congregation Beth B'nai Abraham. This congregation was an offshoot of the early BHI community in Harlem, the Moorish Zionist Temple (1899). The congregation expanded modestly but eventually succumbed to financial failure.[78]

Ford moved to Ethiopia with a group of devoted followers and was present with a delegation at Haile Selassie's coronation. He purchased 800 acres of land to begin the foundation for a Black Exodus from America to Ethiopia. The venture failed. It is unclear what happened to Ford. Some sources say he died in Ethiopia. Other accounts say that under the presumed name Fard, he returned to the United States to start a new religious and cultural Black Nationalist group. The contention was that Fard founded what is now the Nation of Islam. Fard mysteriously disappeared around 1935, and Elijah Muhammad

---

[77] (Klinger, 2020) p7

[78] (Sundquist, 2009) p116-117

took over the leadership of the Nation of Islam. A central cultural element of the Nation of Islam is that the Children of slavery are the chosen people, and Europeans, especially Ashkenazi Jews, are evil.

African Hebrew Israelites of Jerusalem
Founder: Ben Carter also known as Ben Ammi Ben Israel
Date: 1963
Website: http://africanhebrewisraelitesofjerusalem.com/
Location: Dimona, Israel
God: Yahweh
Philosophy: African Hebrew Israelites of Jerusalem

In the 1960s, Ben Carter, also known as Ben Ammi Ben Israel, established the African Hebrew Israelites congregation in Chicago, Illinois. Carter believed the Israelites of the Bible were Jacobites and had claimed over Israel as their homeland. Following unsuccessful resettlement in Liberia, Carter and over 40 families of about 300 BHI from Chicago moved to Dimona, Israel on temporary visas. They claimed their rights under the *Israeli Law of Return*. They chose to remain and fight extradition. The Israeli Rabbinate investigated the claim and concluded that Carter and his community were not Jews. The legal standoffs continued for about 40 years. Due to insufficient citizenship, they lacked the medical and dental capabilities to properly care for one another. Consequently, Carter agreed to support the Israeli military, allowing their young men to fight against the Palestinians in exchange for much-needed supplies for their camp.[79]

Years of discussions and negotiations with the Israeli government over settlement led to their eventual Israeli citizenship in 1990. Now the group numbers around 5,000 and is well-integrated into Israeli society. They have a vegan diet, they speak Hebrew, and their foundation is based on **Jeremiah 23:7-8**

"Therefore, behold, the days come, saith the Lord, that they shall no more say, The Lord liveth, which brought up the children of Israel out of the land of Egypt; 8 But, the Lord liveth, which brought up and which led the seed of the house of Israel out of the north country, and from all countries whither I have driven them; and they shall dwell in their own land."

They are still not recognised as Jews, instead as Israelis. They serve in the Israeli army and have frequently conflicted with Israel over their support for the Palestinian cause.

---

[79] (Klinger, 2020) p7-8

Their views go back to the origins of the BHI and the supposition that the European Jews of Israel are foreigners and were never the true Jews. The European Jews being foreigners and not the true Jews is also a significant plank of Palestinian anti-Israel propaganda and Palestinian efforts to de-legitimise Jewish Israeli settlement.[80]

Apparently, the Israeli government provides special financial consideration and support to Carter's community. They also provide child support, social security, aid to the elderly, disabled, and supplemental income to Dimona's BHI. The Israeli Ministry of Education subsidises the schooling for their children. However, the Israeli governments' refusal to recognise Carter's community as Jews, even after repeated Rabbinic and court investigations, has only exacerbated American Jacobites' feelings against Israel.

The Nubian Islamic Hebrews
Founder: Dwight York
Date: 1967
Location: New York, then Georgia
Philosophy: Numerous: Judaism, Islamic, Christianity, Egyptology, Native American and Extra-terrestrial

Dwight York founded the *Nubian Islamic Hebrews community*, also known as the *Ansaru Allah* (Ansarullah) community, the *Ancient and Mystic Order of Melchizedek*, the *Nuwaubian Nation of Moores*, the *Yamasee Native American Tribe* and currently the *Holy Tabernacles Ministry*. Dwight York himself had many names and titles, including Dr. Michael Z York, Dr. Malachi Z or Melchizedek York, chief Black eagle, Rabboni, Y'shua, Imaam, Isa Abdullah and many others.[81]

York began his first mission in 1967 in Brooklyn, New York. Following a traditional Sufi brotherhood of the larger Muslim world. Wearing Muslim clothes in Black Tunics for men, and veils for women, conveyed the newly embraced Islamic identity.

In 1969, the community focused on Africa and emphasised its ancient Egyptian/Nubian origins accordingly. The group began to wear African robes and was renamed Nubian Islamic Hebrews. In 1970, the community established itself formally in Brooklyn. The

---

[80] (Pinn, African American Religious Culture: Volume 1 A-R, 2009)

[81] (The United Nuwaubian Nation of Moors, 2001)

Nubian Islamic Hebrews had a communal living compound. York traveled to Sudan returning in 1972 to teach about the Sudanese Mahdi, of whom York claimed spiritual and genealogical descent.[82]

In 1992, York again shifted the movement and established the ancient mystic order of Melchizedek with a Nubian connection to the patriarch, Abraham. This focus was solely on the first Hebrew Abraham and not his descendants, the Israelites, rather Ishmael and his son Kadar. In 1993, the group was renamed again and became the United Nubian Nation of Morse, claiming a connection between the native American tribes of the Yamasee and the ancient Egyptians. This narrative was based on a migration that happened before the continental drift from the Nile Valley to the Georgian countryside. The group consisting of 400 members relocated to Georgia, where they became known as the Yamasees.[83]

At one point, York prophesied that a spacecraft from an alien planet would come, on May 5, 2003, to take a chosen 144,000 Nubians to a new planet waiting for their rebirth. However, the mother planet plane never arrived. York was later accused of child molesting and sentenced to 135 years.[84]

Israeli School

Founder: Ebner ben Yomin also known as Abba Bivens
Date: 1969
Location: New York
God: Yahweh
Philosophy: 12 Tribes doctrine. Blacks and Native Indians of the Americas are Israelites

Ebner ben Yomin, also known as Abba Bivens, was initially taught he was an Israelite by an ex-slave years earlier, in the South. Bivens believed in the Black Christ, and on his way to New York, had visited many Indian reservations, and he came to the scriptural conclusion that the native Indians were Israelites. Eventually, in New York, he joined the commandment keepers under Matthews but rejected Matthews' teachings of the old testament only and developed a more negative view of normative Judaism.

---

[82] (Bailey, 2006)

[83] (Times, 2002)

[84] (The United Nuwaubian Nation of Moors, 2001) (Times, 2002)

Bivens founded the Israeli School in 1969, after the "12 tribes" doctrine. Branded as One West, or 1West, due to its address in Harlem, the group became a dominant extremist BHI voice. Bivens was the first to teach both the Jacobites and Native Indians of the Americas are Israelites.[85]

House of Judah
Founder: William A. Lewis
Date: 1969
Location: Chicago, then Michigan
God: Yahweh
Philosophy: William A. Lewis established the House of Judah in Chicago and then relocated to Grand Junction, Michigan. There was an allegation of a beating death of a 12-year-old boy in his House of Judah camp. As per Lewis, *"it was the will of God."*[86]

The Nation of Yahweh
Founder: Hulon Mitchell Jr. also known as Yahweh Ben Yahweh
Date: 1979
Website: http://www.yahwehbenyahweh.com/
Location: Miami, Florida
God: Yahweh
Philosophy: Splinter of UPK, Nation of Islam and BHI ideology.

Hulon Mitchell Jr., also known as Yahweh ben Yahweh, established the Nation of Yahweh, proclaiming himself god, the son of god. He, and many of his followers, were arrested for murder, racketeering, arson and many other crimes they commited in order to establish themselves in various states. He was found guilty of these crimes in 1991 and died of colon cancer in prison. The Nation of Yahweh is perhaps well known for a string of murders in the 1980s. Members were guided by teachings of both the Nation of Islam and BHI ideology that developed into a Black Nationalist movement.

Mitchell is the son of a Pentecostal minister and had joined the nation of Islam before establishing his community, the Nation of Yahweh. According to their official homepage, the nation has managed to amass a 250-million-dollar empire. It has disciples, followers

---

[85] (History of Hebrew Israelism, Intelligence Report, Issue Number: 131, Fall 2008)

[86] (Michigan, 2013)

and supporters in over 1300 cities in the US and in 16 foreign countries. The members of the nation of Yahweh perceive themselves as descendants of the ancient Israelites. They keep Shabbat, relying on the King James Version of the Bible as their holy book, and they believe their spiritual leader, Mitchell, to be the grandmaster of all the gods of the universe, the grand potentate, the everlasting Father and the persecuted Messiah, the son of god.[87]

Mitchell leads probably one of the most controversial BHI groups and is usually classified as a cult movement. Its headquarters, originally in Miami, Florida, was involved in many conflicts with the US government, especially the FBI, in 1990. Yahweh and sixteen followers were indicted on charges of murder in the 1990s, and he was convicted in 1992. The group was responsible for at least fourteen murders that occurred between 1981 and 1990.[88] Members were accused of committing racially motivated murders at Mitchell's request or of furthering the Nation of Yahweh's mission. At trial, members of the organisation testified that Mitchell preached racial hatred and violence, which current members claim to have abandoned.[89] After serving his sentence, which the members interpret as a crucifixion, Mitchell was set free, however he died in 2007.

Another member of this camp, Maurice Woodside, also known as Michael the Black Man or Michael Symonette, was involved in the murder trials. He is a pro-Trump activist with Blacks for Trump[90] in Miami, Florida. Woodside and Blacks for Trump promoted Donald Trump for re-election during the 2020 elections. Woodside posted a video to social media calling President Trump *"the greatest president we have ever had."*[91]

Israeli Church of Universal Practical Knowledge
Founder: Moshe Ben Chareem also known as Mashah
Date: 1973
Website: https://thecomforter.info
God: Yahweh
Philosophy: Splinter of UPK - Nation of Islam and BHI ideology

---

[87] (Pinn, African American Religious Culture: Volume 1 A-R, 2009)

[88] (NYTimes, 1990)

[89] (News F., 2007)

[90] (Bever, 2017)

[91] (Bever, 2017)

Moshe ben Chareem, also known as Masha, was chosen to teach in place of Abba Biven with Peter Sherrod, also known as Yaiqab (who died in 1996). They took over the Israeli School, adding UPK (universal practical knowledge). The name changed several times to re-brand, especially after a failed prophecy of Christ's return in 2000. The new name is the Israelite Church of God in Jesus Christ, Inc. The new leader, an Apostle and Chief High Priest, Tazadaqyah, born Jermaine Grant, rose to power after Ahrayah, one of Biven's disciples, prophesied Christ's return in 2000 to "slay or enslave" all the Edomites (whites) failed to come to pass.[92] His followers knew Tazadagyah as the Comforter, a direct reference to the Holy Spirit, which he spreads on his website.[93]

According to the beliefs of the Israelite Church of God in Jesus Christ, and its offshoots on the famous twelve-tribe chart, the twelve tribes of Israel have their order listing, along with their respective national identities. Judah: American children of slavery. Benjamin: West Indian Blacks. Levi: Haitians. Simeon: Dominicans. Zebulon: Guatemala to Panama. Ephraim: Puerto Ricans. Manasseh: Cubans. Gad: Native American Indians. Reuben: Seminole Indians. Asher: Colombia to Uruguay. Naphtali: Argentina/Chile. Issachar: Mexicans. They also believe the Edomites are the European and that they are cursed. They also preached that the USA's founding fathers were Black and that many other prominent historical figures were BHI, including George Washington, Abraham Lincoln, Thomas Jefferson, King George III, Christopher Columbus, etc.[94]

Five more participants assisted them later in the 1970s, and the Seven Heads were their new name.[95] The Rosicrucians offered them several million dollars to teach a more Christian or Ashkenazi Jewish message of unity for all humanity, as the other Israelite camps taught. Masha and Yaiqab allegedly refused. Accordingly, they believed that a Christian / Jewish message meant the children of slavery would remain on the bottom of society, and the full truth will never be taught.

The House of David
Founder: Moshe Ben Chareem also known as Mashah
Date: 1995

---

[92] (Ready for War, Intelligence Report, Fall 2008)

[93] (The Comforter, 2018)

[94] (The Comforter, 2018)

[95] (History of Hebrew Israelism, Intelligence Report, Issue Number: 131, Fall 2008)

Website: https://hodc12.webs.com/ahic.htm
Philosophy: Splinter of UPK

Ahrayah and Mashah split, even though Ahrayah was the leader of the ICUPK. He made the mistake of teaching that Mashah was King David reincarnated. Thus, when Mashah left, he took many people who believed he was the reincarnation of King David, with him. Mashah's new group was called the House of David; he died in 1999, and the group split into more groups.

Cultural Centre of New Covenant Church of Israel
Founder: Yachov Ben Yisrael
Date: 1996
Website: http://www.thencci.com/
Location: Atlanta, Georgia
God: Yahweh
Philosophy: Ben Yisrael establishes the NCCI (New Covenant Church of Israel) in Atlanta, Georgia.

Israelite Church of God in Jesus Christ
Founder: Jermaine Grant also known as Tazadaqyah
Date: 2000
Website: http://www.thecomforter.info/main/
Location: Harlem
God: Yahweh
Philosophy: Splinter of ISUPK

Jermaine Grant, also known as Tazadaqyah, assumed control of ISUPK and renamed it the Israelite Church of God in Jesus Christ. He claims he is the Holy Ghost/the Comforter, teaching new members that the archangel Gabriel taught him the scriptures on Mount Sinai. They also teach that the mother of Christ was impregnated by the Holy Ghost.[96] Maintaining the legacy and activities of the founding Israeli School, the Israelite Church of God in Jesus Christ continues to operate in Harlem, until recently under the leadership of the late Jermaine Grant, also known as Chief High Priest. Grant was referred to as the Holy Spirit and The Comforter, as he asserted he carried the Holy Spirit within his earthly body.

---

96 (The Comforter, 2018)

In 2013, leader Grant sued a toymaker, Emil Vicale, claiming that the figurine was "not Black enough" and had warped characteristic.[97] An FBI raid in November 2016 produced evidence that Grant and treasurer Lincoln Warrington were stealing money from the organisation and its members.[98] In January 2020, Grant and another member were convicted of using ICGJC funds to unlawfully back their activities. They stole more than $5.3 million from the organisation and its members. Grant was individually charged with defrauding the United States through his tax crimes. He was sentenced to 18 months in federal prison. He died on April 1, 2020, while waiting to begin serving his sentence. While the official cause of death is unknown, the Israelite Church of God in Jesus Christ released a statement that Grant died of COVID-19.[99]

David Anderson and Francine Graham, the perpetrators of the December 10, 2019 attack on a kosher market in Jersey City, New Jersey, had links to the ICGJC. Anderson and Graham deliberately targeted the market and Anderson posted negative content to social media before the attack. Following the shooting, the building administrator of the Israelite Church of God in Jesus Christ, the Harlem location, identified Anderson and Graham as church attendants from four years prior. Social media pages belonging to Anderson are linked to BHI. Anderson claimed he was not a member of an established group and expressed his distrust of such organised camps.[100]

Israel United in Christ (IUIC)
Founder: Nathaniel Ray also known as Bishop Nathanyel Ben Israel
Date: 2003
Website: http://www.israelunite.org
Location: New York
God: Yahweh
Philosophy: Splinter of UPK

Israel United in Christ (IUIC) was founded in New York, in 2003, as a splinter organisation of the Israeli School of Universal Practical Knowledge. Founder, Nathaniel Ray (also known as Bishop Nathanyel Ben Israel), a former member of the One West camp, has built

---

97 (SIEMASZKO, 2013)

98 (Two New Jersey Men Arrested For Evading Taxes On $5.3 Million Taken From New York Religious Organization, 2018)

99 (Controversial leader of Hebrew Israelite movement from N.J. dies of coronavirus, church says, 2020)

100 (James Barron, 2019)

the organisation into an international entity since its inception. Israel United in Christ has 71 locations in the United States and is expanding its international presence with 20 foreign locations.

On August 4, 2018, in Memphis, Tennessee, IUIC members organised the 800-person "Violence Must Stop" march through Memphis to protest incarceration and denounce violence in Jacobite communities. Israel United in Christ has been linked to two acts of violence and has tried to distance itself from the perpetrators. The group publicly rejects any claims it is a hate organisation or advocates violence, but its teachings prove otherwise.

1. In the UK, the East London branch was thrust into the news, in 2018, when a female member, 20-year-old Joy Morgan, disappeared. Morgan, a student and active IUIC member from 2015 until her death, went missing in December of that year following a church activity. On December 26, 2018, Shohfah-El Israel dropped Morgan off at her student housing. Morgan was never seen alive again. In August 2019, Shohfah-El Israel was convicted of her murder and sentenced to 17 years in prison. Morgan's body was not found until October 5, 2019, ten months after she had gone missing.[101]
2. Gerald Duane Lewis, also known as Gaddiell Ben Israel, shot and robbed Crystal Raquel Cash, a transwoman, in Evansville, Indiana in 2016. Cash told law enforcement that Lewis used homophobic slurs during the shooting. After the shooting, IUIC released a statement confirming that Lewis was a member, but he was removed from the organisation for not following guidelines. He pleaded guilty to one count of attempted murder in December 2018.[102]

On August 31, 2019, in Chicago, Illinois, IUIC members held the *IUIC Men's Conference 2019* in Chicago and organised a march attended by 1,000 individuals. According to their website, in addition to keeping a weekly Saturday Sabbath, they also keep the New Moon:

"The new moon is the full moon. The moon was made on the fourth day of creation. The moon rules the night and is for signs and seasons."[103]

---

101 (News, 2019)

102 (Gootee, 2016)

103 (The New Moon is the Full Moon, 2021)

It should also be noted the IUIC fashions itself after freemasonry. There are several YouTube videos depicting IUIC marching with Freemasons.[104] Another YouTube video goes into details, describing IUIC's foundation and exposing their masonic roots[105] and their Masonic attire, for instance, the V-shaped sash, apron, and fringes. It should also be noted the IUIC was registered as an Islamic corporation.[106] On another website dated January 3, 2021, they were registered as a Christian entity.[107]

The Israelite School of Universal Practical Knowledge

Founder: General Yahanna, also known as John Lightborne
Date: 2006
Location: Upper Darby, Pennsylvania
Philosophy: Splinter of UPK

The Israelite School of Universal Practical Knowledge (ISUPK)is a splinter group that changed its original name to Israelite School in 2006. The Israelite Church of God in Jesus Christ (ICGJC) is the modern entity of the original group. ISUPK believes they are the only true BHI group due to their One West roots. The ex-One West General Yahanna, also known as John Lightborne, leads the group. The current iteration of ISUPK operates as a non-profit in Upper Darby, Pennsylvania. There is a particular focus on bringing their ideology to Jacobites communities to end poverty, drug addiction, crime and other social ills.

True Nation Israelite Congregation

Date: 2010
Website: Truenation.org
God: Yahweh
Philosophy: Splinter of UPK - True Nation Israelite Congregation, also known as True Nation is a Californian based faction of the ISUPK and has spread nationally since the early 2010s. They have embarked on trips abroad to establish international connections.

"Truenation.org gives lessons regarding the knowledge of God and his glorious son Yahawashi (Jesus Christ) to the fact that the TRUE children of Israel will be edified."

---

104 (IUIC JOINED WITH THE FREEMASONS?!?!? IUIC SOLD OUT!!!! , 2020)

105 (IUIC FREEMASONRY CONNECTION (GDASH THE PROPHET IS BACK) , 2019)

106 (ISRAEL UNITED IN CHRIST INC, 2020)

107 (ISRAEL UNITED IN CHRIST INC, 2021)

Sicarii Hebrew Israelites
Philosophy: Splinter of UPK

Sicarii Hebrew Israelites, also known as The Sicarii, also known as **Exodus 17:15**. Sicarii's name is from the Israelite Zealots who rallied against the Roman occupation. Originally a California-based group, the organisation has established camps in 10 US cities.

"We are a spiritual community organisation dedicated to the uplifting of disenfranchised, so-called Blacks, Hispanics, Latinos & Native Americans. Through the spirit and power of the Most-High God in the name of his only-begotten Son (YAHAWAH BAHASHAM YAHAWASHI). Teaching the truth of the Bible and reintroducing the lost sheep of the house of Israel to their true identity."

Israelites Saints of Christ (ISOC)
Philosophy: Splinter of UPK

"Our mission is to wake up the so-called Blacks and Hispanic Natives to their true Biblical nationality and cause them to truly follow God in Christ."

"We are a Bible-based organisation that teaches repentance to the Twelve Tribes of the nation of Israel. Our goal is to spread this marvellous truth throughout the earth. The So-Called Negroes and Hispanic Natives are the True Biblical Israelites."

The Law Keepers
Date: 1997
Website: http://www.thelawkeepers.org/
God: Yahweh
Philosophy: Belief in the entire Old Testament from Genesis to Malachi known as the *Tanakh*

The Law Keepers was founded in 1997 as a BHI movement of Torah-only Hebrew Israelites. The law-keepers have made it their primary purpose to:

"Exalt honour and give praise and glory to the only one of Yishrael YHWH, return to the land of their forefathers and the land of Yishrael. Also, to assist and act as an advocate for like-minded Hebrews, Yishraelites who have returned to their heritage and who desire to return to their homeland."

The law keepers do not embrace the *New Testament* and reject *Yeshua* (Jesus) as their saviour. They believe in the entire Old Testament from Genesis to Malachi, known as the *Tanakh*, and the book of the prophets. They keep the Shabbat and celebrate the

Ashkenazi Jewish holidays. The law keepers perceived themself as the descendants of the biblical tribe of Judah, which according to their historiography had been taken into captivity and exile during the Grecian Empire. The community calls for an exodus from the Americas and aims at returning to their putative ancestral homeland Israel.

The Law keepers seek to accomplish their objective by claiming reparation payments from the US government to assist with their relocation to the holy land. According to the law keeper's homepage, they have established a community in the Hashemite Kingdom of Jordan. Being rejected under the Law of Return to Israel, the law keepers found an alternative location in Jordan that welcomed them with an open-door policy. The move resembles returning to their ancestral homeland, as Israel's ancestral day boundaries fell within Jordan. In Jordan, the Law Keeper aimed at establishing a community involving housing, farmland, a health clinic, and a school.

House of Israel
Founder: Kani Zabach
Website: They have a Facebook page
God: Yahweh
Philosophy: Splinter of UPK

HOI was founded by leader Kani Zabach, who studied at Harlem's One West Camp, in New York. The organisation has many US branches and engaged in activities with other BHI organisations, including street teaching and networking conferences.

"Community organisation that actively participates in uniting and building up the nation destroyed by Colonialism, Imperialism, and Slavery."

"Call back to the fold the Blacks, Hispanics, and Native Americans; who are the Twelve Tribes of Israel. Through Edification, News, and Practical Knowledge sharing."

Two notable groups go by the name House of Israel. There is one in Ghana that is currently corrupted by the Ashkenazi Jewish practices. The Ghanaian HOI reached out to the Israelite Nation World Wide Ministries in the early 90s, and at the time, their practices were more scriptural based. However, shortly after that initial contact, the Ghanian HOI was contacted by an Ashkenazi Jewish organisation, Kulanu Inc., and now they practice Judaism. This group has pretty much infiltrated all of the self-professed Israelite groups in Africa and other countries except for any Western hemisphere groups.

There is another HOI which is in Guyana, South America. The Guyanese HOI was established by an American fugitive, David Hill, also known as Rabbi Edward Washington, who arrived in Guyana in 1972. This faction of the HOI is reminiscent of the Back to Africa movement of the BHI, and they use Israeli Hebrew terms. Bernard Darke, a British-born, Guyanese Jesuit priest and photographer for the *Catholic Standard*, was stabbed to death in 1979 by members of the HOI. As a result, the Guyanese HOI is often compared to the notorious 1978 cult led by the Reverend Jim Jones, of Oakland, California. They were well known for the mass murder-suicide at the commune of the People's Temple of Christ, in Guyana.

Zabach accused Edomites of staging the shooting to ridicule the BHIs and published this in a video in December 2019. He further claims the shooting was a message from God, that the 'Edomite detective' Joseph Seals was killed for violence against the Jacobite community. Israelites should not feel sympathy towards the 'three so-called Jews' slaughtered, again claiming that the attack could be fake.

Members of the House of Israel have been recognised as having antagonised high school students, at the Lincoln Memorial in Washington DC in January 2019, for attending an anti-abortion rally. The incident gained national coverage when a student was accused of taunting an American native elder. The Kentucky students' parents sued multiple news outlets for defamation; others ended up in settlements, including the Washington Post and CNN. It was later revealed HOI members were taunting the students and Native Americans with racial slurs and chants.

Also, in Miami, Florida, in October 2019 , after reportedly attacking two people at a temple, Larry Greene, alias Elijah Israel, was charged with an exacerbated attack with a lethal weapon. Green is a self-identified BHI adherent, not affiliated with an existing sect, suggests 'fake Jew' ought to 'go back to Israel.'

Notable Mentions

The Church of Israel
Website: http://www.thecoi.com/

Hebrew Israelite Heritage
Website: http://www.hebrewisraelites.org/

The Shield of Wisdom
Website: http://www.shieldofwisdom.com/

The True Branches of Christ
Website: http://www.truebocc.com/index.htm

Israelite Board of Rabbis, Inc.
Website: http://www.blackjews.org/

List of Black Hebrew Israelites
Website: http://www.inetmgrs.com/hebrew/Temple_Listings/temple_listings.html

Chapter Eight

Spiritual Identity

The Israelite Nation World Wide Ministries (INWWM) is not affiliated in any way with the Black Hebrew Israelites (BHI) or their affiliated identity. The INWWM is not affiliated with Masonic Christianity, Freemasonry, Mind Power, Theosophy, Judaism, the occult, or any other philosophy.

The INWWM teaches that there is a thin line between the lie and the truth in terms of spirituality. With the naked eye, things that appear to be Godly are not and similar instruments and methods that many organizations and established individuals may use are also used to serve the God of Truth, the God of Abraham, Isaac and Jacob. Their practices go against the creed and codes of conduct of the Israelite Doctrine. For one, none of the INWWM's leaders or teachers make claims to predict the future, yet they are taught to recognize the unfolding or fulfillments of biblical prophecies.

None of the leaders receive any payment whatsoever for the services they provide, which may include, but are not limited to, teaching, conducting spiritual services, counselling, preparation and setting up of the place of worship etc. As a matter of fact, the leaders of the INWWM make great sacrifices to perform the services of God for their fellow brethren. For instance, taking time off work, waking up early hours of the morning, or cancelling personal family time to attend a feast, fast and pray, or to prepare the environment for a service or feast. They do whatever is necessary to assist a brethren in dire need and for the upliftment of the nation.

Participants are always encouraged to do their own research and ask questions or seek advice. The INWWM prides itself as being a teacher of all nations and has taught people from a diversity of backgrounds, race, colour and creed. But what is not taught is miracles, healing and obtaining of great wealth, even though this may be implied in the messages received and biblical accounts. The doctrine is spread through music, art, theatre, worship, lessons, bible studies, etc. This gospel of truth allows people of all nations to understand the Israelite doctrine and share in the rich culture and heritage.

However, participants are not encouraged to take the steps towards baptism and becoming a brethren.

As a matter of fact, people are often discouraged from taking the step towards Baptism; this is such an integral step in a person's life and understanding that as a person is only born once, they can only be baptized once. It is therefore important that a person undergoing this process be of sound mind and have reasonable understanding of the doctrine, to be baptized. Thus, there is no coercion, threats, pressure, duress, intimidation, oppression, blackmail, preaching of hell and damnation, promises of health, wealth and prosperity, no path of succession or assurance of heavenly riches.

BHI is also known as African Hebrew Israelites, Black Jews, Black Hebrews, Black Israelites, or Hebrew Israelites. BHI is an umbrella term for various Black activist sects and congregations that believe that people of colour, usually Jacobites, the Children of Slaves, are descendants of the lost tribe of the biblical Israelites. BHI does not consider all people of colour to be part of the lost tribes. As one BHI website explains, "Israel is just one black nation that exists among many. The Egyptians, Canaanites, Ethiopians, Babylonians etc., were black-skinned, but they were not Israelites. To say all black-skinned people are Israelites is like saying all Asians are Chinese, or All Europeans are French."

The three largest BHI groups are the International Israelite Board of Rabbis, the Church Of God And Saints Of Christ – Temple Beth El, and the African Hebrew Israelites of Jerusalem. They are all affiliated in one way or the other, receiving similar foundations and instructions. As they are called, all other camps are splinters of the Universal Practical Knowledge, a spinoff from the Israeli School, founded by Ebner ben Yomin, also known as Abba Bivens, which began as a Black Nationalist movement in the late 1960s. Most BHIs affirm the King James Version (1611) of the Bible as their only rule of faith and practice.

However, some BHI does not accept the books of the Second Testament, while others accept them but reject the teachings of Paul because the white slave masters used them during American slavery. The irony is that although the BHI does not accept the second testament, they use the word *Rabbi*. Rabbi is a word found in the second testament and attributed to Jesus the Christ himself **"But be not ye called Rabbi: for one is your Master, even Christ; and all ye are brethren." Matthew 23:8.** Bishop and King are also names used by some camps.

Most, if not all, BHI groups deny the Trinity and the deity of Christ. They believe that there is a distinction between God and Jesus of Nazareth, where God is the Supreme Being and Jesus a human being. However, all of them refer to Yahweh or Elohim, or some variation, which technically speaking would be their god's name. Not all BHI groups align themselves with Judaism. Some adopt traditions and ideas gathered from a wide range of other sources including Masonic Christianity, Freemasonry, Mind Power, Theosophy, Judaism, the occult and of course the Israelites from the Old Testament. Some are even associated with the Ethiopian Jews (aka Beit Yisrael or Falashas), such as the New York's main body of BHI, who called themselves Ethiopian Jews from the 1930s to 1960s. Egypt and Ethiopia were often regarded as Israel's enemies, and Israel often did battle with them, as noted in **2 Chronicles 16: 8. "Were not the Ethiopians and the Lubims a huge host, with very many chariots and horsemen? yet, because thou didst rely on the LORD, he delivered them into thine hand."** So it is a wonder why one would want to turn to Egypt or Ethiopia, for these were not the nations chosen by the God of Israel.

Even though many BHI camps will deny that they are fashioned after Judaism, they wear tassels at the end of their garments calling them fringe. Others wear aprons with tassels like the Masonic Christian order. Recently, a group of BHI placed a blue ribbon above their fringe. Talking about blue ribbons, anyone would recognise the INWWM's flag with its vibrant colours of blue, red, white and purple, as described in **Exodus 25:4**, however, keeping with the Back to Africa theme, the BHI adopt the Black and green for their colours. These are not Israelite Colours, and those nations that have taken the Israelite colours of blue, red, white and purple are predominately the progressive nations. Those countries that hold dear the colours of Africa, namely the Black and the green, are not so advanced – see for yourself.

BHI are so physical in their understanding that their women do not wear trousers, yet in biblical times women and men wore a dress like those in the Middle East or Asia and all over the scriptures speaks of skirts for instance; **Psalm 133:2, "It is like the precious ointment upon the head, that ran down upon the beard, even Aaron's beard: that went down to the skirts of his garments."** They even vehemently preach against men not having beards, yet many do not follow the laws of circumcision, one of the fundamental aspects of an Israelite male.

When it comes to the Physical Identity, most BHI members agree that the Israelites were Black and that the God they serve was Black. Nevertheless, this quickly started to change as some believe that Israelites are gentiles, and the 'white-man' including the 'Ashkenazi Jews' are from Esau. The story becomes even more muddled when it comes to the so-called 'Hebrew Language'.

The BHI's holy days, for the most part, are synonyms with the teachings of Judaism and most of them look for the first crescent moon to begin their monthly countdown, all have a recurring weekly sabbath which they call Shabbat. One HBI camp believes that the full moon is their new moon. It is not certain how they would calculate the Passover from this though, nevertheless, if the foundation is false, so are the premises.

As we have discovered, most BHI members, especially those who end up in power, change their birth names. Changing names is the custom of the Israeli people that have usurped God's chosen people's identity. However, as we have noted earlier, Jacob was the last Hebrew. His name was changed to Israel, not by his mother or father, but by the God of Israel himself. Therefore, all of his descendants were known as Israelites. Just a note, the Muslims of America change their names on joining the organisation. The Catholics are also huge fans of changing names; this is why they have conformations for little girls and boys. They are given a Catholic name – they obviously understand the spiritual connotation that this practice has.

A few important things should be noted here. While the Jacobites have always strived to embrace an identity, none of the teachings within these BHI camps has been revolutionary; especially after the early insurrections. The Back to Africa movement did not necessarily start with Marcus Garvey; however, he was responsible for making it popular, even though Garvey never returned to Africa. Furthermore, not only are women not allowed to teach, BHI does not understand the women's role. The BHI keep missing the part mentioned in Isaiah, that we would be a light to the Gentiles. Some believe that they are gentiles while others think that all people with white skin, which is to say gentiles and Esau, are cursed and would not allow them to join their organisation. Yet, our edict, as per **Matthew 28:19**, is is to teach all nations as in

The transatlantic slave trade not only resonates, but it was a continuation of the Spanish and Portuguese inquisition and the plight of our Israelite forefathers. In the mid-1980s Porter began to document an even deeper connection prophesied in Genesis, Deuteronomy and Isaiah. While many people over the last few hundred years recognised the correlation between Moses leading the children of Israel out of Egypt and the transatlantic slave trade, Porter spoke in-depth, rigorously and often about the 400 years of slavery that the children of Israel had in store for them during our modern times.

The 400-year narrative was recorded in every book Porter wrote and every speech he gave since he first stumbled on this revelation. He even went as far as looking at the state of countries like Egypt, Spain, Portugal and even Africa, deciphering the cause of their current state. The empirical evidence is that none of those countries has regained their former glory because of what they did to the Children of Israel. Right now, the whole world is watching with bated breath to see what would become of the New Egypt, which is the United States of America. Since the ending of the 400 years, for Israelites that was Adar (February) 2020, and along with the crazy politics, the whole world has been under-siege by a great plague known as COVID-19 and while no man knows what tomorrow brings, as Israelites we do understand that this was prophesied.

Today the market is swamped with books on the topic of Israelite Identity. Porter was one of the first to take a deep dive into the Journey of the Israelites, identifying his God, culture, physical identity, spirituality and history. But it is no surprise that many have greedily helped themselves to the information he shared and have flooded the market with all kinds of ad-hoc theories and regurgitated a great deal of his work, without acknowledging the source of their knowledge.

Yet, there is a great deal of information that only a baptised brethren of the INWWM are privy to such as, the Christ, The Disciple that Jesus loved, the True Sabbath Day and New Moon, the meaning of Isaiah 19, the New Egypt, secrets of the double triangle, the Importance of Water, the Israelite colours and many more. Elder Shadrock Porter's revelations inspired these teachings. As he slowly unravels some of these mysteries to the world, we can see who has been listening, like Nicodemus creeping around in the dark pursuing knowledge. Except they will never say where they got their information. It is a wonder as to how many people that have heard these teachings, understand the magnitude, depth and scope of these Revelations.

Conclusion

This work began while compiling a list of the various Black Hebrew Israelite camps that exist and the genesis of their existence. However, something was missing. It was essential to provide some background narrative that may affect the BHI's fundamental beliefs, like the biblical Israelites being Black, the belief in a black God and the belief of the prophecy in **Deuteronomy 28:68**. This shared understanding was encouraging, as it demonstrated a colossal breakaway from the iron-clad clutches of Christianity. However, it is difficult to understand why the BHI publicly ridicule and express their disdain for the Ashkenazi Jews while at the same time adopting his customs, dress and especially his language, hence the section on 'Speaking Hebrew.'

Another puzzling aspect of some HBI camps was the Back to Africa movement. As a result, it was necessary to write about Africa and her fundamental involvement in the slave trade. There were so many unanswered questions, like exactly how the Israelites settled in West Africa, since East and Central Africa are far closer to Jerusalem? According to the holy covenant, the Israelites would be punished for turning away or forsaking their God, the God of Israel. So what were the Israelites practising? How come so many tribes in Africa have Israelite customs? Why did one Black man sell another? After several unplanned discussions with various Israelites and years of research, the visualisation of the Israelites and their existence in Africa started to materialise. These questions and more were answered throughout this book.

The INWWM may be a "very small remnant," as mentioned in Isaiah, nevertheless, they continue to reach for and achieve great things. Even becoming a Nation within a Nation, with their constitution, flag, coat of arms, way of life, all this and more sets them apart and has afforded them a presence on the world stage where they can glorify the God of Israel and show their appreciation to the Master Teacher.

The Hidden Secret of the True Israelites is our Spirituality and the God whom we serve. Our God, the God of Abraham, the God of Isaac and the God of Jacob is merciful, compassionate, loving and just. He is to be feared, He is supreme and perfect, the Alpha and Omega, the first and the last, the beginning and the end. He is the creator and redeemer, oath keeper, life-giver, the Father of the Israelites. Those that worship him must do so in Spirit and Truth, and those that claim to love Him must keep His Commandments. It is that simple.

We are his chosen People, the Israelites.

Bibliography

(2018, 3 28). Retrieved from The Comforter: https://thecomforter.info

Bailey, J. H. (2006). The Final Frontier: Secrecy, Identity, and the Media in the Rise and Fall of the United Nuwaubian Nation of Moors. *Journal of the American Academy of Religion - Oxford University Press.*

Bever, K. M. (2017, 8 23). *The strange story of that 'Blacks for Trump' guy standing behind POTUS at his Phoenix rally.* Retrieved from Washington Post: https://www.washingtonpost.com/news/morning-mix/wp/2017/08/23/the-strange-story-of-that-blacks-for-trump-guy-standing-behind-potus-at-his-phoenix-rally/

Blanc, H. (1968). The Israeli Koiné as an Emergent National Standard. *Language Problems in Developing Nations*, 237-252.

Bleich, J. D. (1975). *"Black Jews: A Halakhic Perspective". Tradition: A Journal of Orthodox Jewish Thought.* Rabbinical Council of America (RCA).

Boyarin, D. (2016). *The Christian Invention of "Judaism".* California: University of California at Berkeley.

Chafets, Z. (2009, April 2). *Obama's Rabbi.* Retrieved from The New York Times Magazine: https://www.nytimes.com/2009/04/05/magazine/05rabbi-t.html

COGASOC. (2020, 11 2). *Prophet William S. Crowdy.* Retrieved from Church of God and Saints of Christ: https://www.cogasoc.org/leaders/prophet-william-s-crowdy/

Controversial leader of Hebrew Israelite movement from N.J. dies of coronavirus, church says. (2020, 4 13). Retrieved from NJ.com - True Jersey: https://www.nj.com/coronavirus/2020/04/controversial-leader-of-hebrew-israelite-movement-from-nj-dies-of-coronavirus-church-says.html

Dalby, A. (2015, 10 28). *Dictionary of Languages: The definitive reference to more than 400 languages.* Retrieved from Google Books: https://books.google.ca/books?id=7dHNCgAAQBAJ&dq="Hebrew+ceased+to+be+an+everyday+spoken+language"&source=gbs_navlinks_s

Eugene V. Gallagher, W. M. (2011). *Introduction to New and Alternative Religions in America.* . University of California Press .

EurekAlert. (2010, 1 7). Retrieved from Most Ancient Hebrew Biblical Inscription Deciphered: https://www.eurekalert.org/pub_releases/2010-01/uoh-mah010710.php

Fellman, J. (2020, 7 28). *Hebrew: Eliezer Ben-Yehuda & the Revival of Hebrew.* Retrieved from Jewish Virtual Library: https://www.jewishvirtuallibrary.org/eliezer-ben-yehuda-and-the-revival-of-hebrew

Gallagher, E. V., & Ashcraft, W. M. (2006). *Introduction to New and Alternative Religions in America.*

Gootee, R. (2016, 7 12). *Evansville shooting suspect identifies with alleged hate group.* Retrieved from Evansville Courier and Press:

http://archive.courierpress.com/news/crime/evansville-shooting-suspect-identifies-with-alleged-hate-group-376f773c-362f-68d7-e053-0100007fe86a-386475291.html/

HaaretzAP. (2008, 10 30). *Have Israeli Archaeologists Found World's Oldest Hebrew Inscription?* Retrieved from Haaretz Associated Press: https://www.haaretz.com/1.5052529

Hinds, E. M., & Castrilli, E. T. (1995, December 29). *The Spirit of Egypt in America.* (E. S. Porter, Ed.) Toronto: Fifth Ribb Publishing.

(Fall 2008). *History of Hebrew Israelism, Intelligence Report, Issue Number: 131.* Southern Poverty Law Center.

History.com. (2017, 6 6). *Slave Rebellions.* Retrieved from History.com: http://www.history.com/topics/black-history/slavery-iv-slave-rebellions

Identity and Power. (1992, January 15). *Elder Shadrock & the Children of the Prophets.* Toronto, Ontario, Canada: Fifth Ribb Publishing.

Israel United In Christ Inc. (2020, 11 28). Retrieved from 501c3lookup: https://501c3lookup.org/lookup=4104a1a5b1dbf7cdf166a9b53fa00d98

Israel United In Christ Inc. (2021, 1 3). Retrieved from TaxExemptWorld: https://www.taxexemptworld.com/organization.asp?tn=1516910

IUIC Freemasonry Connection (Gdash The Prophet Is Back) . (2019, 10 30). Retrieved from YouTube: https://www.youtube.com/watch?v=mB8zwvRGMzY

IUIC Joined With The Freemasons? IUIC SOLD OUT!!!! . (2020, 6 1). Retrieved from YouTube: https://www.youtube.com/watch?v=6rYRqrerVh4

Izre'el, S. (n.d.). *The Emergence of Spoken Israeli Hebrew.* Retrieved 2020, Oct, 28, from https://www.tau.ac.il/~izreel/publications/Emergence_Hary2003(corr).pdf

James Barron, M. G. (2019, 12 11). *Jersey City Shooting: Suspect in Attack Wrote Anti-Semitic Posts.* Retrieved from New York Times: https://www.nytimes.com/2019/12/11/nyregion/david-anderson-francine-graham-jersey-city.html

Johnston, H. H. (1910). *The negro in the New World.* London: Macmillan.

JUNE 23, 1923: Marcus Garvey's Trial Ends; He Has Been Sentenced To A Five-Year Imprisonment. (2019, 6 4). Retrieved from Black Then: Discovering Our History: https://blackthen.com/june-23-1923-marcus-garveys-trial-ends-sentenced-five-year-imprisonment/

Kaplan, K. (2014, 9 9). *DNA ties Ashkenazi Jews to group of just 330 people from Middle Ages.* Retrieved from The Los Angeles Times: https://www.latimes.com/science/sciencenow/la-sci-sn-ashkenazi-jews-dna-diseases-20140909-story.html

KJV. (1611). *King James Version Bible.*

Klinger, J. (2020, 11 15). *The Black Hebrew Israelites and Kansas.* Retrieved from Jewish American Society for Historic Preservation: http://www.jewish-american-society-for-historic-preservation.org

Kotlawī, A. Y. (n.d.). *Akhlāq-uṣ-Ṣāliḥīn.* Karachi, Pakistan: Maktaba-tul-Madīnaĥ.

Koestler, A. (1976). *The Thirteenth Tribe* .

Konighofer, M. (2008). *The New Ship of Zion: Dynamic Diaspora Dimensions of the African Hebrew Israelites of Jerusalem.* LIT Verlag Munster.

Krauskopf, J. (1887). *Jews and the Moors in Spain* . https://archive.org/details/jewsmoorsinspain00krauuoft/page/218/mode/2up?q=heaven+ : M. Berkowitz & Company.

Levy, R. S. (2017, 8 28). *The Destruction of Commandment Keepers, Inc 1919-2007.* Retrieved from Black Jews.: http://www.blackjews.org/Essays/DestructionofCommandmentKeepers.html,

Mahajan, D. (2008, July 22). *Yahweh.* Retrieved from Britannica: https://www.britannica.com/topic/Jehovah-2108642

Marcus Garvey (1887 - 1940). (2020, 9 17). Retrieved from BBC History: http://www.bbc.co.uk/history/historic_figures/garvey_marcus.shtml

Martin, T. (2009, 10 21). *Marcus Garvey.* Retrieved from Religions: https://www.bbc.co.uk/religion/religions/rastafari/people/marcusgarvey.shtml

Michigan, M. L. (2013, 6 28). *House of Judah: Prophet's son denies father led a cult or enslaved children.* Retrieved from M Live Michigan: https://www.mlive.com/news/grand-rapids/2013/06/house_of_judah_prophets_son_de.html

Mujaddid, E. A. (2020, 1 12). *The 1899 Moorish Zionist Temple founded (3 decades) after the United States Civil War.* Retrieved from Murakush Society Inc: https://murakushsociety.org/the-1899-moorish-zionist-temple-founded-3-decades-after-the-united-states-civil-war/

Myers, E. A. (1987). *The Eerdmans Bible Dictionary.* Grand Rapids, Michigan: Wm. B. Eerdmans Publishing Co.

News, B. (2019, 10 10). *Joy Morgan murder: Woodland body confirmed as student.* Retrieved from BBC News: https://www.bbc.com/news/uk-england-beds-bucks-herts-49998305

News, F. (2007, 5 8). *Temple of Love' Black Supremacist Cult Leader Yahweh Ben Yahweh Dies at 71.* Retrieved from Fox News: http://www.foxnews.com/story/2007/05/08/temple-love-black-supremacist-cult-leader-yahweh-ben-yahweh-dies-at-71/

NYTimes. (1990, 11 08). *F.B.I. Arrests Members of Black Sect in 14 Slayings.* Retrieved from New York Times: https://www.nytimes.com/1990/11/08/us/fbi-arrests-members-of-black-sect-in-14-slayings.html

Ogilby, J. (1670). *Africa: Being an accurate description of the regions of Egypt, Barbary, Lybia and Billedulgerid: Section III: The Visible Empire.* London: Johnson.

Pike, A. (1871). *Morals and Dogma of the Ancient and Accepted Scottish Rite of Freemasonry* . Montana, USA: Kessinger Publishing Company.

Pinn, A. B. (2009). *African American Religious Culture: Volume 1 A-R.* Westport, CT: Greenwood Publishing Group. Retrieved from https://jude3project.org/blog/2016/2/3/overview-of-the-black-hebrew-israelites

Porter, E. S. (1991). *The Forgotten Israelite*. Toronto: Fifth Ribb Publishing.

Porter, E. S. (1993). *The Word, the Israelites, and the Damned*. Toronto: Fifth Ribb Publishing.

Porter, E. S. (1995). *The Truth, The Lie and The Bible* (Third ed., Vol. Third Edition). Toronto, Ontario, Canada: Fifth Ribb Publishing.

Porter, E. S. (2000). The Spirit, The Passion and The Blood: A Nicky Porter Story. Toronto: Fifth Ribb Publishing.

Porter, E. S. (2019, August 24). Speech For The 400-Years Seminar . Fort Monroe, Virginia.

(Fall 2008). *Ready for War, Intelligence Report*. Southern Poverty Law Centre.

SIEMASZKO, B. R. (2013, 4 25). *Harlem church sues toymaker Emil Vicale after talking doll in leader's likeness is not black enough*. Retrieved from New York Daily News: https://www.nydailynews.com/new-york/harlem-church-suing-leader-doll-not-black-article-1.1327823

Sundquist, E. J. (2009). *Strangers in the Land: Blacks, Jews, Post-Holocaust America*. Harvard University Press.

The New Moon is the Full Moon. (2021, 1 28). Retrieved from Israelite United in Christ: https://israelunite.org/high-holy-days-3/the-new-moon/

The United Nuwaubian Nation of Moors . (2001, 1 11). Retrieved from Sniggle: https://sniggle.net/dave/Reviews/review009.html

This We Believe. (2020, 10 28). Retrieved from Church of God and Saints of Christ: https://www.cogasoc.org/about/this-we-believe-2/

Times, W. (2002, 2 2). *Nuwaubian Nightmare*. Retrieved from Washington Times: https://www.washingtontimes.com/news/2002/jun/2/20020602-030741-8461r/

Toby Widdicombe, J. M. (2017). *Historical Dictionary of Utopianism*. Rowman & Littlefield.

Two New Jersey Men Arrested For Evading Taxes On $5.3 Million Taken From New York Religious Organization. (2018, 4 25). Retrieved from Justice.gov: https://www.justice.gov/usao-nj/pr/two-new-jersey-men-arrested-evading-taxes-53-million-taken-new-york-religious

Wikipedia. (2009, 7 7). *Israel*. Retrieved from Wikipedia: https://en.wikipedia.org/wiki/Israel

Wikipedia. (2020, 12 1). *Beth Shalom B'nai Zaken Ethiopian Hebrew Congregation*. Retrieved from Wikipedia: https://en.wikipedia.org/wiki/Beth_Shalom_B%27nai_Zaken_Ethiopian_Hebrew_Congregation

Wikipedia. (2020, 9 28). *Hebrew Language*. Retrieved from Wikipedia: https://en.wikipedia.org/wiki/Hebrew_language

Wikipedia. (2020, Nov 3). *Ilah*. Retrieved from Wikipedia: https://en.wikipedia.org/wiki/Ilah

Wikipedia. (2020, Nov 3). *Yahweh*. Retrieved from Wikipedia.

Wikipedia. (n.d.). *William Saunders Crowdy*. Retrieved from Wikipedia: https://en.wikipedia.org/wiki/William_Saunders_Crowdy

www.ingramcontent.com/pod-product-compliance
Lightning Source LLC
Chambersburg PA
CBHW062140100526
44589CB00014B/1637